Written at a time when news can be fake and facts can have alternatives, this book provides teachers with innovative research-based instructional strategies that help students learn how to think through complex questions in a deliberate and informed way. It is a timely and valuable resource for practitioners who are looking for effective ways to address a pressing educational priority: teaching students how to critically evaluate various types of information and reach a sound conclusion. Importantly, the book treats teachers as co-inquirers, who reflect on their own thinking and continue to learn with their students.

Alina Reznitskaya, Professor, Department of Educational Foundations, Montclair State University, New Jersey

In this brief volume, Dr. Sanacore provides a desperately needed reprieve from the onslaught of teaching guides that focus on "delivering content" and scalability, and guides us through some of the ways we can help to foster more critical engagement from our students. Some of the specifics here are likely to be familiar to those who have teaching experience—indeed, some of them have been used over millennia in one form or another—but even the most experienced teachers will find something useful to draw on and to help improve not what their students know, but how they know. It is the sort of book you keep nearby when you need a reminder of what is important about teaching, and how you can contribute to the lives of your students and to our broader discourse through your choices in the classroom.

Alexander Halavais, Associate Professor of Data & Society, New College, Arizona State University

Teaching Critical Thinking in the Context of Political Rhetoric

During the past several decades, there has been a blitz of information, sometimes referred to as the knowledge explosion, and students have struggled in their attempts to distinguish true, fake, and terribly biased information, especially regarding political issues. This book highlights the value of critical thinking as a way to navigate this difficult and frustrating terrain, so that students grow and develop as knowledgeable, independent thinkers. To promote this growth, the book offers thoughtful, evidence-based advice for teachers to support students' deep thinking as it relates to real-world contexts. Strategies presented include student reflection based on experience, moving from narrow to broader perspectives, and using graphic organizers to build and activate knowledge before, during, and after instructional activities. With the instructional guidance and activities presented in this short, easy-to-apply volume, teachers can give students the tools they need to negotiate the often-murky waters of political communication.

Joseph Sanacore is a journalist, researcher, and professor in the Department of Teaching and Learning at the Post Campus of Long Island University, Brookville, NY. He has authored more than 100 articles, essays, and book chapters. He was also an elementary, middle, and high school teacher and a K–12 Director of Language Arts and Literacy.

Teaching Critical Thinking in the Context of Political Rhetoric

A Guide for Classroom Practice

Joseph Sanacore

NEW YORK AND LONDON

First published 2022
by Routledge
605 Third Avenue, New York, NY 10158

and by Routledge
2 Park Square, Milton Park, Abingdon, Oxon, OX14 4RN

Routledge is an imprint of the Taylor & Francis Group, an informa business

© 2022 Joseph Sanacore

The right of Joseph Sanacore to be identified as author of this work has been asserted by him in accordance with sections 77 and 78 of the Copyright, Designs and Patents Act 1988.

All rights reserved. No part of this book may be reprinted or reproduced or utilised in any form or by any electronic, mechanical, or other means, now known or hereafter invented, including photocopying and recording, or in any information storage or retrieval system, without permission in writing from the publishers.

Trademark notice: Product or corporate names may be trademarks or registered trademarks, and are used only for identification and explanation without intent to infringe.

Library of Congress Cataloging-in-Publication Data
Names: Sanacore, Joseph, author.
Title: Teaching critical thinking in the context of political rhetoric : a guide for classroom practice / Joseph Sanacore.
Description: New York, NY : Routledge, 2022. | Includes bibliographical references.
Identifiers: LCCN 2021018696 (print) | LCCN 2021018697 (ebook) | ISBN 9781032079707 (hardback) | ISBN 9781032079691 (paperback) | ISBN 9781003212300 (ebook)
Subjects: LCSH: Critical thinking--Study and teaching. | English language--Rhetoric--Study and teaching. | Rhetoric--Political aspects.
Classification: LCC LB1590.3 .S248 2022 (print) | LCC LB1590.3 (ebook) | DDC 370.15/2--dc23
LC record available at https://lccn.loc.gov/2021018696
LC ebook record available at https://lccn.loc.gov/2021018697

ISBN: 978-1-032-07970-7 (hbk)
ISBN: 978-1-032-07969-1 (pbk)
ISBN: 978-1-003-21230-0 (ebk)

DOI: 10.4324/9781003212300

Typeset in Palatino
by MPS Limited, Dehradun

To my five delightful grandchildren (in chronological birth order): Gabriel, Spencer, Darien, Nathan, and Cayden. May you always have a zest for seeking the truth and thinking critically. I love you guys with all my heart and soul.

Contents

Easing into the Book x

1 Introduction 1
2 The Need to Teach Critical Thinking 10
3 Promoting Critical Thinking 13
4 Application and Transfer of Learning 32
5 Other Strategies and Activities That Support Transfer of Learning 71
6 The Value of Hard Work 80
7 Reflections on Critical Thinking 84
8 In Retrospect 101
   References 105
   About the Author 117

Easing into the Book

Joseph Sanacore

Politicians are expected to be positive role models for children, adolescents, and adults, and what they say and do represent leadership behavior. Regrettably, some political leaders have demonstrated negative behavior in both rhetoric and actions. Because citizens are observing such behavior, they might believe it is okay to emulate it. Teachers therefore must accept a vitally important, but delicate, role of teaching critical thinking skills without imposing teacher biases. In the context of political rhetoric, students need guidance to analyze, synthesize, apply, evaluate, and problem-solve creatively because this instructional direction will help them to grow and develop as knowledgeable, independent thinkers. While focusing on these and other aspects of higher interactive thinking skills (HITS), insights are inspired by the foundation work of Bloom, Engelhart, Furst, Hill, and Krathwohl (1956), by *The Foundation for Critical Thinking* (2019), by Vanderbilt University's Center for Teaching (Armstrong, 2020), by Willingham (2019), by state education department standards, and by spiritual theorists, researchers, and practitioners.

Moving in this direction is the major goal of this humble book. Although classroom teachers and school administrators have been promoting critical thinking nationwide, their efforts are sometimes limited and are missing essential ingredients that consistently support HITS. Part of this gap between good intentions and inadequate implementation is caused by confusion about how to define critical thinking, how to develop a supportive rationale, and how to apply its tenets across the curriculum.

Furthermore, if teachers are expected to foster critical thinking in their students, they, themselves, must be critical thinkers, they must be deep thinkers, they must have intellectual humility, and they must have a reasonable, rational, multi-logical worldview. "In short, teaching for critical thinking presupposes a clear conception of critical thinking in the mind of the teacher" (Paul & Elder, 2007). Without such dispositions, teachers might be building, instead of tearing down, barriers to foster critical thinking.

While not a panacea, the book highlights the value of critical thinking and its connection to subject content because this instructional approach is substantially more effective than teaching critical thinking in isolated or generic ways. Moreover, no holier-than-thou, or superior, approach has been imposed on teachers. Instead, thoughtful strategies and activities are suggested that teachers might consider useful when addressing the purposes and objectives of content areas as well as the interests, strengths, and needs of students. This teaching-learning environment provides opportunities for connecting both direct instruction and student-centered approaches across the curriculum so that students can apply critical thinking skills to interesting and meaningful contexts, thereby increasing transfer of learning. An important reminder to both educators and students is that teaching critical thinking is most beneficial when it aids humanity and is driven by spiritual and moral commitment.

The "Introduction" provides a warmer-upper for valuing critical thinking. While providing a spiritual and earthly foundation for this important part of school curricula, critical thinking is initially defined via *The Foundation for Critical Thinking*. During the past several decades, there has been a blitz of information, sometimes referred to as the knowledge explosion, and students need support distinguishing among true, fake, and terribly biased information. This perspective is considered in a broad, inclusive context because political rhetoric is used not only by politicians but also by others with questionable motivations.

"The Need to Teach Critical Thinking" offers support for nurturing students' higher interactive thinking without imposing teacher bias, either directly or subtly. Furthermore, as social media platforms and Artificial Intelligence technologies allow "virtually" anyone to develop fake audio and video, students need support as they attempt to understand these problematic substructures and questionable motivations.

"Promoting Critical Thinking" focuses on students immersed in a variety of print and media sources as they learn about political rhetoric versus fact finding. Multifaceted aspects of reflection, based on experience, are discussed as well as the necessity of broadening perspectives instead of relying on limited experiences and reflections. Suggested criteria for effective lesson plans support students' efforts to further understand aspects of critical thinking, especially when the lessons are geared specifically to content areas. Supporting this instructional direction are important conditions of literacy learning that need to be considered. Additionally, examples of blank graphic organizers are useful tools for structuring information related to research on political rhetoric. As students engage in listening, speaking, reading, writing, and visualizing, they sometimes access loads of confusing information, and they understandably have difficulty determining true facts from fake news. The graphic organizers presented in this section are only a sampling of available instructional tools for structuring, clarifying, and evaluating rhetoric.

In "Application and Transfer of Learning," teachers support students' efforts to further understand critical thinking and to apply this deeper way of thinking to varied content. As students connect higher interactive thinking across the curriculum, they appreciate the value of transfer of learning. Meaningful examples with transfer value include channel-surfing; ThinkCERCA platform; productive group work concerning the 1935 Social Security Act; sports and society class; pairing of easy and challenging books; pairing of traditional books, graphic books, and film versions; use of quality literature to promote inference making with young children; painting writing and writing painting context;

reflective practice and service learning; immigrants, jobs, and crime; independent reading, vocabulary development, and comprehension; creativity and problem solving; humor and creative problem solving; universities, corporate models, and whistleblowing; and propaganda devices.

"Other Strategies That Support Transfer of Learning" continues to provide students with experiences that extend their critical thinking skills to meaningful contexts. Learners benefit substantially from ongoing experiences, in which they apply HITS to different venues. Among the supports to consider are inquiry dialogue, open-ended and inclusive questions, more wait time for deep thinking, and learning journals.

"The Value of Hard Work" presents several studies that support the efficacy of a rigorous learning environment that is stimulating, engaging, and challenging. This type of school climate can narrow the achievement gap between ethnic minority learners and their more advantaged peers and can motivate all students' work ethic for attaining success.

In "Reflections on Critical Thinking," the challenge of nurturing students' growth as critical thinkers is elaborated. Both teachers and students need to persevere because this type of growth represents a considerable shift in learners' values and attitudes. Among the areas on which to reflect are the challenges of political partisanship, the practical implications of understanding these challenges, the importance of cooperation, the value of intrinsic motivation, and the need for de-stressing before engaging in HITS and their application to novel settings.

"In Retrospect" is a reminder that as students show empowerment to think critically, they initially might experience discord because learning to take a new road to thinking requires leaving behind old, ineffective ways of thinking. Supporting this mission can situate teachers as "divine craftspersons" who nurture critical thinking as a spiritual service that blends theoretical and spiritual awareness with practical experience. A complementary consideration is to connect deep thinking to Buberian I-Thou relationships, which can result positively in treating people with full spiritual respect. Regardless of the varied perspectives, this growth-oriented, psycho-spiritual journey receives evidence-based support that values connections among critical thinking, content-oriented learning, and a balance of direct instruction and student-centered experiences. Retrospectively and introspectively, highly competent and caring teachers will inspire students to embrace and apply HITS to personal contexts, to politics, and to domestic, national, and international issues.

Finally, the listing of "References" not only provides documentation but also symbolizes a sense of reading the past so we can write the future. This is in line with UNESCO's stance.

I hope you enjoy this humble book and find it useful in your classroom practice as you and your students embrace the value of critical thinking as part of your daily existence.

1
Introduction

"... I think that sometimes life and language break each other open to change, that a rupture in one can be a rapture in the other, that sometimes there are, as it were, words underneath the words–even the very Word underneath the words" (Wiman, 2016). Writing in *The American Scholar*, Christian Wiman's (2016) reflection is spiritually inclined, and it has value for understanding the varied meanings of words and their empowering potential for changing people's beliefs, for better or for worse. In the political context, words in the form of rhetoric have dominated politics in all countries for thousands of years, reflecting both positive and negative motivations. Some politicians, religious leaders, philosophers, news anchors, journalists, salespersons, neighbors, and others have used words to lie, exaggerate, exploit, bully, and promote bigotry. This broad, inclusive perspective suggests that the words *political* and *rhetoric* are used not only by politicians but also by others with questionable intent. Words can be used to "grab attention, manipulate emotions, and sneakily win arguments when you are backed into a corner. Ultimately, rhetoric provides a means to magnify your cause. It can be used for good or evil ... I encourage students to use it for good" (Building Critical Thinking, 2013). When negative motivations occur, however, they often generate alternative facts, as the average citizen sometimes struggles in varied attempts to distinguish fake news from factual content. Aristotle (1924/2011, p. 203) believed that although the intent of rhetorical speech was "to lead to decisions," not all speakers are credible and trustworthy. Aristotle observed that sophistic rhetoric, for example, "deliberately used misleading arguments and ambiguous words to deceive the listeners. When used this way, discourse no longer communicates wisdom; rather it obfuscates and deceives the public" (Minin-White, 2017, p. 14). Because language and power can manipulate and influence the world (Freire, 2000), this reality instigates a call to action to teach critical thinking so that citizens—old and young—have opportunities to interpret the rupture of language and to experience the rapture of becoming rational, independent thinkers.

In this book, critical thinking is often referred to as higher interactive thinking skills (HITS) because it is hard to imagine deep thinking without engaged communication for processing and interpreting meaning in any venue. Furthermore, although definitions and interpretations of critical thinking abound, *The Foundation for Critical Thinking* (2019) provides commonalities for understanding and applying this essential part of school curricula:

> Critical thinking is that mode of thinking—about any subject, content, or problem—in which the thinker improves the quality of his or her thinking by skillfully analyzing, assessing, and reconstructing it. Critical thinking is self-directed, self-disciplined, self-monitored, and self-corrective thinking. It presupposes assent to rigorous standards of excellence and mindful command of their use. It entails effective communication and problem-solving abilities, as well as a commitment to overcome our native egocentrism and sociocentrism.

Complementing this definition is Elfatihi's (2017) rationale for teaching critical thinking skills. Although it focuses on language teaching for ESL (English as a Second Language) and EFL (English as a Foreign Language) students, the rationale is applicable to all learners because virtually everyone is a language learner. According to Elfatihi,

1. Philosophically, critical thinking is connected to language and thought;
2. Cognitively and metacognitively, critical thinking influences and is influenced by processes, including comprehension, memory, and metacognitive awareness;
3. Pedagogically, instructional strategies and methodologies often require engagement in processing

information, solving problems, making decisions, and evaluating results;
4. Socioeconomically, critical thinking is useful and pragmatic in social and interpersonal contexts, and the same perspective is needed to access the job market and to be successful in it.

Critical thinking is also essential for building a solid foundation in teaching and learning because "Much of our thinking, left to itself, is biased, distorted, partial, uninformed, or down-right prejudiced. Yet the quality of our life and that of which we produce, make, or build depend precisely on the quality of our thought" (Paul & Elder, 2007). As educators support the use of critical thinking in their classroom practice, they need to highlight the fundamental purpose of fostering traits of mind because "intellectual traits or dispositions distinguish a skilled but sophisticated thinker from a skilled fair-minded thinker. Fair-minded critical thinkers are intellectually humble and intellectually empathic. They have confidence in reason and intellectual integrity. They display intellectual courage and intellectual autonomy" (Elder & Paul, 2010, p. 38).

There are a range of critical thinking dispositions (CTDs) that are identified in professional literature. They include: inquisitiveness, open-mindedness, self-efficacy, attentiveness, intrinsic goal orientation, perseverance, organization, truth-seeking, creativity, skepticism, reflection, and resourcefulness. Of these 12 categories, research findings suggested "that the most influential of CTDs were inquisitiveness, open-mindedness, and self-efficacy, whereas the CTDs most enhanced by other dispositions were reflection and resourcefulness" (Dwyer, 2019; see also Dwyer, Harney, Hogan, & Kavanagh, 2016).

These dispositions suggest that effective critical thinking is neither value-neutral nor merely instrumental because it is deeply and personally connected with values and attitudes. Concerning values, making effective judgments or evaluations of problems requires not only an evaluative basis for decision-making but also a challenge of the values on which the judgment is made. Thus, effective critical thinking involves thoughtful reflection and analysis of values before they are accepted. It also increases the potential that critical thinkers and their perspectives will be challenged and may be changed. This reflexive context further supports connections between critical thinking and attitudes because it suggests growth in maturity, independence, and openness to consider and understand different perspectives. "Critical thinking, then, is not a merely logical exercise, but is a practice richly imbued with a set of values and attitudes" (Lynch, n.d.; see also Bartlett, 1932; Nord, 1995).

Supporting critical thinking and encouraging related dispositions are especially needed today because people have easy access to a blitz of information from their cell phones, iPads, laptops, and other technological devices. This blitz has resulted in "ideological bubbles" as people tend to pursue information sources that reflect their values and opinions (Bavel & Pereira, 2018), thereby hindering an understanding of others' perspectives and opinions (Lombard, Schneider, Merminod, & Weiss, 2020; Rowe et al., 2015). Managing and understanding the increased access to information require critical thinking so that citizens develop the ability to distinguish true from fake or terribly biased information. In his essay "It's Time to Get Serious About Teaching Critical Thinking" (2020b) and his book *Critical Thinking* (2020a), Jonathan Haber provides valuable insights that can be adapted to elementary, secondary, and college settings. Foremost is the application of critical thinking across content areas, resulting in transfer of learning, and this vitally important approach is more effective than teaching critical thinking generically (Willingham, 2019).

As teachers incorporate critical thinking across the curriculum, they come to realize that higher interactive processing requires calm, reflective thinking, and we can gain related insights from the themes and events in children's literature.

In his book titled *Quiet*, award-winning children's writer Tomie dePaola (2018) provides a warm story with beautiful cartoon illustrations—done with transparent acrylics and colored pencils using a muted palette—that show a grandfather and his granddaughter and grandson walking in a park and observing busy aspects of nature. When they decide to sit on a bench and quietly observe and reflect, they realize that being quiet and still is good for thinking and seeing. Metaphorically, the serene context of *Quiet* can be applied to many aspects of life, including the busy rhetoric and actions of politicians and the need for reflection and engagement in critical thinking.

This perspective fits well with current views of how the human brain functions. In Kahneman's (2011) view, briefly described, the brain has two systems that inform our thinking: System 1 represents fast thinking related to visual and cognitive illusions demonstrated through quick impressions, impulses, and intuitions (often in error), whereas System 2 reflects slow thinking related to effort and self-control. Individuals who uncritically adhere to their intuitions are likely to accept suggestions from System 1. "In particular, they are impulsive, impatient, and keen to receive immediate gratification" (p. 48), and they are more likely to believe and appreciate quick, gut-level rhetoric. If children are observing related household dispositions and are not encouraged to disagree in an agreeable manner, they probably will not grow beyond their limited backgrounds, as they undoubtedly will continue to demonstrate comparable feelings and behaviors learned and reinforced during childhood and adolescence. The outcomes are obvious: The next generation of American citizens will lack the ability to think critically and beyond the rhetoric of their favorite political leaders, colleagues, parents, neighbors, friends, and others—with or without moral intent.

Understanding this perspective is essential for navigating today's culture of questionable discourse. In a special issue of

Informal Logic, guest editors Katharina Stevens and Michael Baumtrog (2018) highlighted the theme of "Reason and Rhetoric in the Time of Alternative Facts." The articles in this issue are thoughtful and provocative, and they contribute to a growing awareness of reason and rhetoric in today's culture of politics. Collectively, the articles clarify issues of political fabrications and fake news, and they reinforce the importance of teaching critical thinking in elementary and secondary schools and colleges.

Moving in this direction requires genuine caring with a "big-picture" vision of learning and teaching (Sanacore, 1999). Especially needed is serious holistic attention to students' emotional, social, cognitive, and interactive needs, regardless of their genders, cultures, disabilities, and socioeconomic backgrounds. Thayer-Bacon (1993) clarified this relational epistemology view of caring in her thoughtful essay "Caring and Its Relationship to Critical Thinking":

> People do not have to like or love each other in order to care. They do need to develop the ability to be receptive and open to other people and their ideas, willing to attend to them, to listen and consider their possibilities. Care does NOT entail that people agree with each other. Care does mean that people are open to possibly hearing others' voices more completely and fairly ... Caring about other people ... requires respecting others as separate, autonomous people (ideas, other life forms, etc.) worthy of caring. It is an attitude that gives value to others by denoting that others are worth attending to in a serious or close manner (p. 325).

While caring about students' growth and development, some educators avoid potentially controversial issues (Murray-Everett & Coffield, 2020), even though students need and generally want to learn to deliberate about such issues. As important, this learning experience is powerfully connected to political engagement (McAvoy & Hess, 2013). According to Kolluri (2017/2018), "Democracy necessitates civil deliberation of thorny political issues. If schools, out of fear, neglect to develop this capacity, students will graduate unprepared to navigate political controversies and potentially reluctant to influence the political contexts that shape their lives" (p. 41).

Fortunately, the wave of social justice movements in the United States has resulted in one of the first school systems nationwide to recognize the importance of student activism. The Fairfax (VA) County Public Schools, for example, will allow secondary-level students one excused absence every school year to engage in such civic activities as sit-ins, marches, and trips to lobby legislators. According to Ryan McElveen, Fairfax School Board member, "I think we're setting the stage with this … It's a dawning of a new day in student activism, and school systems everywhere are going to have to be responsive to it" (cited in Natanson, 2019). From a curricular perspective, student activism is passionate and has the potential to engage students in the critical thinking process as a firsthand, lived-through experience.

In support of social justice movements, student activism can be especially effective when it is influenced by moral imperatives and when moral decisions are not only about inspiration but also about pertinent information. In his blog "Research is Vital to the Moral Integrity of Social Movements," Rev. Dr. William J. Barber II (2019) noted that factual information forces society to realize the harm and the hurt of decisions people are making. "We've seen too many movements that have bumper sticker sayings but no stats and no depth. Researchers help to protect the moral integrity of a movement by providing sound analysis of the facts and issues at hand."

Barber II's perspective is well received. Before students engage in activism, they should be encouraged to conduct research to determine the efficacy of the social justice movement they intend to support. A related problem that is pervasive, however, is that not enough children, adolescents, and adults are thinking critically in their daily lives. They seem to be more comfortable accepting fake facts that support their comfort zone, especially when this incorrect information is connected to their limited perspectives and cognitive biases (Anson, 2018; Azarian, 2018; Dunning, 2011, 2016; Kahneman, 2011; Kruger & Dunning, 1999; Nilson, 2018). Educators therefore need to accept the responsibility of and commitment to promoting critical thinking as an educational priority and a practical reality (Haber, 2020a, 2020b). These efforts need the support of school administrators, classroom teachers, teacher-educators, professors, policymakers, mission statements, and, of course, professional development sessions that highlight not only the application of evidence-based practices but also the nourishment of educators' inner life (Intractor & Kunzman, 2006).

Such support is becoming increasingly evident in professional organization position statements and in state education department standards. The National Council for the Social Studies, for example, released a Media Literacy position statement in 2016 that indicated, "While print literacy continues to be a key priority in K-12 schools, there is a growing consensus that this new [media] information landscape requires new approaches to teaching and learning. Our discipline has an opportunity to lead the way in teaching students to both analyze and produce rich, complex, diverse and engaging mediated messages" (NCSS, 2016). Also supporting students' engagement in critical literacy skills is the NCSS (2013) *College, Career, and Civic Life (C3) Framework for Social Studies State Standards: Guidance for Enhancing the Rigor of K-12 Civics, Economics, Geography, and History.*

2
The Need to Teach Critical Thinking

Encouraging critical thinking of controversial topics is especially needed today as some politicians exploit Americans who desire a better future for their families. Teachers must therefore assume a vitally important, but delicate, role as they nurture students' analytical and critical thinking skills without imposing teacher biases on their students. Granted, virtually everyone has biases in favor of or against certain individuals, places, and things. Teachers need to be keenly aware of their own biases and to not directly or subtly sway students toward accepting them. "Although teachers should express their own opinion if asked, they should not try to lead students to the conclusion they themselves have reached" (Noddings & Brooks, 2017, p. 12). This stance is particularly important when teaching about potentially controversial topics and themes, such as political discourse versus factual reality. According to Sulzberger (2018),

> Powerful forces are stoking distrust in the news media with attacks on the press and sowing confusion by promoting clickbait, rumor, and fraudulent stories and propaganda. This has been driven in no small part by various politicians and technology platforms pursuing their short-term interests over the greater good. These tactics contribute to growing polarization and undermine trust in news organizations (p. A2).

Not surprisingly, social media are one of the most powerful sources that can influence public opinion, and Artificial Intelligence technologies can make it easy for "virtually" anyone to create fake audio and video (Borel, 2018). As students continuously encounter such manipulation of and by the media, they are challenged to infer the difference between credible information and disinformation. Understanding this difference is vitally important because we do not want to encourage students to become lifetime pessimists who mistrust all media. Eroding trust in all media sources dissuades students from engaging in the hard work of collaborating with peers to pursue the truth.

Educators can support this type of collaboration by stressing the value and application of critical thinking in developmentally appropriate ways so that children and adolescents become better thinkers and citizens in their daily lives. Embracing this context makes sense because human beings have extraordinary abilities that can result in creative restlessness, which "beats and pulsates what is most deeply human: the search for truth, the insatiable need for the good, hunger for freedom, nostalgia for the beautiful, and the voice of conscience" (John Paul II, 1979). As students are guided in collaborative dialogue, their "creative restlessness" can be morphed into cohesive and coherent outcomes that promote a zest for determining truth and for supporting social justice through efforts that bring about an open mind and a will to the demands of the common good (Benedict XVI, 2005; see also Bonagura, 2019).

3
Promoting Critical Thinking

As teachers support higher interactive thinking skills (HITS), they should be admirable role models who embrace Socrates's warning by helping students to realize that true knowledge is not simply organized information; instead, it is a collection of facts that has been analyzed with the guidance of moral criticism (Noddings & Brooks, 2017). Moreover, Plato believed that there are truths to be realized, that truth is objective, and that when we use our reason correctly, we can apprehend truth. Plato also believed that we have a three-part soul: appetitive (appetites or urges), spirited (emotional), and rational. The moral soul is the just and harmonious soul, which is guided by reason and keeps the appetitive and spirited parts in alignment (Vaughn, 2017).

Teachers can motivate students to pursue true knowledge through reviews, debates, role-play, historical reenactments, mock trials, and mock interviews of politicians' rhetoric via their speeches, tweets, media interviews, press conferences, and other communication sources. During these participatory activities, students are encouraged to demonstrate independence and objectivity as they engage in higher-level thinking that involves comparing and contrasting political rhetoric with factual content from credible sources. Supporting this instructional direction is the use of graphic organizers, which help students to structure their listening, speaking, reading, writing, visualizing, notetaking, and other meaningful activities. Types of graphic organizers include semantic maps, concept maps, knowledge maps, compare/contrast matrixes, structured (hierarchical) overviews, and Venn diagrams. Manoli and Papadopoulou (2012) describe these and other graphic organizers and their connections to research, teaching, and learning. (See examples of graphic organizers at the end of this chapter.)

When students engage in activities related to the topic of political rhetoric versus fact finding, they can clarify and organize their thoughts by using a Venn diagram, named after John Venn (1880). The Venn diagram consists of two or three interconnected circles: one for the rhetoric, one for the facts, and one for agreement between the rhetoric and the facts. This supportive tool is useful when collecting and organizing information from a variety of print and media sources.

The Media

Because students are in front of the screen about six hours a day (IRA Inspire, 2012; Sanacore & Piro, 2014), they profit from assignments in which they gain information from television and Internet websites. Working cooperatively in pairs or in small groups, they have opportunities to compare and contrast information from media outlets, which can increase their awareness that major broadcast networks like ABC, CBS, and NBC are mostly moderate; that MSNBC is mostly liberal; that CNN attempts to present both sides of an issue; and that Fox News is mostly conservative. Similarly, students' experiences with other media and print sources help them to interpret a variety of perspectives, ranging from liberal to conservative. These sources include *The Washington Post*, *The New York Times*, *The Nation*, *The New Yorker*, *National Public Radio*, *Slate*, *Politico*, *The Economist*, *Wall Street Journal*, *Washington Examiner*, *The Weekly Standard*, *City Journal*, *New York Post*, *Breitbart News*, Sean Hannity, and Glen Beck.

Additionally, elementary and secondary school students are avid consumers of YouTube, Instagram, Snapchat, TikTok, Twitter, and Facebook, and these and other social media platforms provide excellent learning opportunities for promoting critical thinking. For students who consistently prefer certain platforms or are reluctant to read or view a traditional source, teachers can expand their repertoire of experiences by motivating them to pair traditional media outlets with the ones they frequently use. For example, while working in small, productive groups, students can observe political debates on TikTok and CNN and then can engage in a comparative analysis of these debates. Pairing these nontraditional and traditional sources can have the same positive effect as pairing young adult literature and challenging books, which are discussed in the "Application and Transfer of Learning" chapter.

Because an increasing quantity of news content is available via social media platforms, they add to our tech-saturated world with popularity and legitimacy (Little, 2018). That said, students need support as they navigate and mitigate diverse issues that follow their digital lifestyle. In responding to a 2018 report of the Pew Research Center, Alex Halavais, who directs the M.A. in Social Technologies program at Arizona State University, advised:

> The primary change needs to come in education. From a very early age, people need to understand how to interact with networked, digital technologies. They need to learn how to use social media, and learn how not to be used by it. They need to understand how to assemble reliable information and how to detect crap. They need to be able to shape the media they are immersed in. They need to be aware of how algorithms and marketing—and the companies, governments, and other organizations that produce them—help to shape the ways in which they see the world (Anderson & Rainie, 2018).

Recognizing the subtle and direct biases of broadcast, digital, print, and social media platforms supports students' growing awareness, sophistication, and independence when dealing with different information sources. These engaging experiences with comparing and contrasting ideas increase students' prior knowledge of content so they can effectively discuss, debate, and share critical papers reflecting their own substantive viewpoints about political leaders and critical issues and trends. Such a balanced perspective gives students opportunities to think critically, to gain ownership of their ideas and opinions, and to develop independence in their thinking processes.

Importance of Reflection

The essence of this learning/teaching context is that students are working together as an integral part of the school curriculum. Shared, *reflective* experiences enrich students' curiosity and critical thinking and motivate them to be valuable citizens who work collectively to make their lives better (Dewey, 1938a, 1938b; Noddings & Brooks, 2017; Sanacore, 2013). The key word is *reflective* because it enhances the value of experiences as it increases the usefulness of critical thinking.

Because true reflection is multifaceted and consists of varied dimensions, let us consider a synthesis of related definitions (Sanacore, 2013): According to Boyd and Fales (1983), "Reflective learning is the process of internally examining and exploring an issue of concern, triggered by an experience, which creates and clarifies meaning in terms of self, and which results in a changed conceptual perspective" (p. 99). In Scott's (2010) empirical study, reflection is defined "as the conscious awareness and questioning of personal experience, a search for alternative explanations and interpretations, and identification of areas for improvement" (p. 430). Supporting this perspective is Mills and Jennings's (2011) teacher-researcher project, in which the central features of inquiry are reflection and reflexivity; that is, reflective dialogue is used to promote reflexivity. Thus, students learn to study themselves so they can outgrow themselves as individuals and as a community of learners. Morawski (2012) highlighted multiple means of engagement with the study of adolescent literature via the practice of resolution scrapbooks, which are reflective and multimodal recordings of a person's response to trauma (Aust, 1981; Lowenstein, 1995). Originally developed to help abused individuals' emotional healing, Morawski used an adaptation of this reflective practice and examined its application to an adolescent novel study. Although Dewey's stance on the importance of reflection was extensive and was elaborated in several publications (Dewey, 1933, 1938a, 1944), he retrospectively viewed this process as not based in experience but instead in *reflection* of the experience. For Dewey, reflection is a progression that requires meaning-making and continuity of learning, systematic and rigorous thinking with a foundation in scientific inquiry, interaction with others, and attitudes that value intellectual and personal growth not only of oneself but also of others (Rodgers, 2002). In ancient Greece, Socrates promoted dialogic learning, which "required attentive listening, critical analysis, careful reflection, and argumentation" (cited in Lotherington, 2011, p. 126). Taken together, these and other definitions of reflection suggest that it is multifaceted and that it requires doing hard work; thinking deeply, analytically, and critically about experience; responding personally to learning; verifying personal responses to learning; being curious and inquisitive; having patience with ambiguity; and connecting these reflective practices so that they are working in concert. This "big-picture" perspective should be considered inclusive and therefore beneficial for all students.

Not surprisingly, when teachers and students engage in reflection through experience, they might encounter failure because this type of deep thinking involves risk-taking. Failure, however, can be an instructive aid for both teachers and students as it indicates further observations need to be made. Those who really think can learn as much from their failures as from their successes because "failure either brings to light a new problem or helps to define and clarify the problem on which [teachers and students have] been engaged" (Dewey, 1933, p. 114). Ultimately, the key players need to keep the faith as they attempt to turn failures into successes. In this context, faith can be described as "the realization of what is hoped for and evidence of things not seen …" and faith helps us to understand that "what is visible came into being through the invisible" (Letter to the Hebrews, 11:1-3, cited in Culp, 2018). Faith also helps us to develop spiritual maturity—not naïveté—and to work harder at removing obstacles to solving problems and, in turn, finding solutions to resolving failures.

Reflective Wallowing

Considering today's quick-paced society and the many ways information is presented, students need opportunities to become immersed in the reflective practice of wallowing as they learn to experience and appreciate varied forms of text that might involve multiple modalities (or sign systems). Because literacy is increasingly multimodal (Kress, 2010) and combines many resources for making meaning (Jewitt & Kress, 2003), learners benefit from support in understanding gesture, movement, speech, music, sound effect, gaze, image, and other modes. As students learn to relax and wallow, they are likely to experience a variety of multimodal text, including **print-based and screen-based texts** (i.e., using both traditional and digital text); **graphic stories** (i.e., increasing comprehension with graphic depictions of setting, characterization, plot, and factual content in a wide variety of books, including Random Riggs and Cassandra Jean's *Miss Peregrine's Home for Peculiar Children: The Graphic Novel* and Don Brown's *Drowned City: Hurricane Katrina and New Orleans*); **performance poetry** (i.e., using poetry that is composed and/or performed before an audience); **animated narratives** (i.e., presenting abstract concepts across the curriculum by developing or compiling narratives with music, video, image, animation, and other multimedia supports); **drawing** (i.e., engaging in naturally and developmentally appropriate activities that enhance meaning); **portraiture** (i.e., learning techniques for drawing the face as a way of students telling their visual stories); **claymation** (i.e., exploring complex concepts with hands-on activities for working tangibly and physically with characters and models);

picture books (i.e., using both the words and the illustrations as equal multimodal partners for pursuing meaning and considering certain picture books as acceptable and respectable for older students); **e-books** (i.e., enjoying quick and easy access to treeless resources, with opportunities to change the font size and to listen to some of the ebooks as audiobooks); **audiobooks** (i.e., building word recognition, comprehension, and fluency by connecting reading with listening as a read-along activity); **art** (i.e., becoming immersed in doing and observing art as a vehicle for intensely analyzing the world with its many layers of meaning); **music** (i.e., appreciating varied musical forms as outlets for individual expression, cooperative group work, and links to lyrical communication); **dance** (i.e., engaging in choreography to generate deeper feelings and interpretations as complements to curricular activities); and **podcast and multimodal media production** (i.e., presenting personal information in visual and audio formats). Even carefully selected video games and computer simulations can "support language development, analytical thinking, critical responses, and other reflective habits" (Sanacore & Piro, 2014, p. 57). When reflective wallowing is not sentimental, it can result in productive thinking as students explore different informational sources and develop substantive viewpoints about content.

Broadening Perspectives

These cooperative, growth-oriented opportunities are vitally important because people have a tendency to narrow their scope of experiences (and related reflections), thereby limiting their viewpoints. In *Thinking, Slow and Fast*, Kahneman (2011) describes a study that has implications for WYSIATI (WHAT YOU SEE IS ALL THERE IS). Although all participants in the study read legal scenarios, different groups were exposed to one-sided presentations about the scenarios, and some participants heard both sides.

The participants were fully aware of the setup, and those who heard only one side could easily have generated the argument for the other side. Nevertheless, the presentation of one-sided evidence had a very pronounced effect on judgments. Furthermore, participants who saw one-sided evidence were more confident of their judgments than those who saw both sides. This is just what you would expect if the confidence that people experience is determined by the coherence of the story they manage to construct from available information. It is the consistency of the information that matters for a good story, not its completeness. Indeed, you will often find that knowing little makes it easier to fit everything you know into a coherent pattern (p. 87).

This limited perspective, however, results in biases of choice and judgment. For example, if students receive news information from only MSNBC and *The Washington Post*, they are likely to experience current events through a liberal lens. Conversely, if learners receive news information from only *Breitbart News* and Sean Hannity, they are apt to experience current events through a conservative window.

In a major report on polarization conducted at the Pew Research Center, Mitchell, Gottfried, Kiley, and Matsa (2014) found that those who are consistently liberal or consistently conservative make up about 20% of the overall public. These two groups have a substantial impact on the political process, as they are most likely to vote, to participate directly in politics, and to donate to campaigns. Additional findings of the study indicate that 47% of consistent conservatives cite Fox News as their major source of news about politics and government. By contrast, consistent liberals use a greater range of news outlets, including *The New York Times* and National Public Radio. Concerning the 2016 presidential campaign, Mitchell, Gottfried, and Barthel (2017) found that Fox News was the dominant news source for Trump voters (40%), whereas CNN was the main news source for Clinton voters (18%).

Students need to broaden their scope of experiences instead of relying on limited, one-sided perspectives. A broader scope informs students of varied information from which they can develop their own substantive opinions based on a synthesis of credible evidence. This potential outcome is more likely to be realized when teachers provide a warm learning environment that considers learners' feelings and emotions. Although these are complex mechanisms for both students and teachers, they can result in positive outcomes when the classroom atmosphere is warm and supportive. Students are more apt to take risks and engage in activities when they feel the learning environment is warm (Sanacore, 2012).

Considerations for Effective Lesson Plans

An important part of this humanistic learning foundation is for teachers to guide and respect students' choices and to immerse them in related conversations that broaden their perspectives (Noddings & Brooks, 2017; Sanacore, 2012). Supporting this instructional direction are effective lesson plans that encourage both choice and pertinent discussions. Because examples of print and digital lesson plans abound, none is provided here. Effective plans, however, consist of the following essentials, but they should not be carried out generically. Instead, they have greater value when they are applied specifically across the curriculum.

- Instructional objectives, cooperatively developed by students and teachers, that clarify students' performance, conditions under which students will perform, and the extent of performance
- Instructional strategies and activities to attain the objectives and the types of support that teachers will provide to ensure success

- Traditional print, digital, and multimodal resources to support the strategies and activities that further ensure successful outcomes
- Enrichment follow-up activities, to be chosen by students, that reinforce the value of thinking critically and independently, for example, informal whole-class and small-group discussions, formal debates and speeches, mock interviews, critical essays, and classroom newspapers in which students create political cartoons (caricatures) and write informational articles, Op-Ed essays, and letters to the editor
- Teacher assessment and student self-assessment to determine cooperatively the degree to which the objectives have been attained.

When these considerations are connected to an instructional lesson or unit concerning political rhetoric, specific factors need to be incorporated into the teaching/learning process. For example, students benefit from an increased awareness of:

- definitions of rhetoric
- biased rhetorical devices ("colorful," emotionally toned words)
- political motivations for using biased rhetoric or language
- elements of logic
- techniques of persuasion
- fact checking
- examples of fallacies or misconceptions.

A deeper understanding of rhetorical techniques is an essential part of a critical thinking toolkit, which will help students to bring a critical edge to political speeches, advertisements, and everyday discussions and will motivate students to interpret more quickly underlying claims, issues, values, and motivations (Building Critical Thinking, 2013).

This expanded view of rhetoric suggests that we need to see beyond illusions that often reflect superficial appearances, deliberately created. Kasten (2017) believes that although the effects might be subtle, they nonetheless can be profound by making us miserable or even killing us:

> We need to know if foods that taste perfectly fine can hurt us in the short term (as with *Salmonella* contamination) or in the long term (cholesterol). A virus might be so dangerous that we should avoid public places, and political candidates promising to clean up government can end up being more corrupt than their predecessors. We want to know if items we purchase are durable or junk, and whether people we're attracted to are truly as considerate as they seem at first. Students are constantly being presented with information not only in the classroom, but also from their friends, parents, the Internet, films, television, radio, newspapers, and magazines. They need tools to analyze all the input (Kasten, 2017; see also Building Critical Thinking, 2013).

Conditions of Effective (Literacy) Learning

As teachers work steadfastly to promote critical thinking, their lessons are more likely to be effective when they are interwoven with important conditions of learning. According to Cambourne (1999), these include immersion, demonstration, expectations, responsibility, approximations, practice, and feedback. When placed in the context of explanations and teacher actions, these seven conditions are more easily understood and applied to effective instructional practices across the curriculum and through the grades. Consider these adaptations applied to critical thinking:

1. Immersion—students need to be immersed in content and context when learning something new. If students

are expected to learn and appreciate advanced thinking skills, the content needs to be meaningful and relevant to their lives.
2. Demonstration—students benefit from teacher demonstrations that are practical and serve as concrete models. Then, require students to do something explicit to demonstrate what they have learned about critical thinking, and motivate them to use multisensory and multimodal approaches.
3. Expectations—clearly identified learning expectations guide every lesson. Encourage students to reach for the highest expectations, and provide a supportive environment for them to do so.
4. Responsibility—strive to have your students become accountable for their own learning. Include problem-solving choices and leadership experiences in your program.
5. Approximations—recognize approximations as students engage in higher-level thinking, and plan learning experiences that are slightly beyond students' current demonstrated abilities. This approach supports learners' reachable potential, for example, their zone of proximal development (Vygotsky, 1978).
6. Practice—students need many opportunities to practice with new knowledge, skills, and attitudes. Gradually change the variables of time, support, place, groupings, complexity, and context to move the new learning toward independent use.
7. Feedback/support/celebrations—feedback should be specific, pertinent, and continuous. Remember that learning to become critical thinkers is challenging, so celebrate successes, provide concrete and realistic feedback, help to set new goals, and plan next steps. (Adapted from Cambourne [1999] and https://www.psd1.org/cms/lib/WA01001055/Centricity/domain/34/ktresources/CAMBOURNES_SEVEN_CONDITIONS_OF_LEARNING.pdf.)

Examples of Graphic Organizers

As teachers consider these and other important conditions of learning, they might use maps, matrixes, diagrams, structured hierarchical overviews, anticipation guides, and other graphic organizers to support effective instruction in critical thinking. Because graphic organizers overlap and vary in format, teachers need to adapt them to the objectives, strategies, resources, and reflections/evaluations of instructional lessons and units. When graphic organizers are connected to meaningful content, these important tools help the human brain to make natural connections to learning, which can clarify and expand rich vocabulary and concept development. This process reinforces the brain's capacity for understanding and remembering important content, skills, and strategies and then applying them to novel settings, resulting in transfer of learning. As a cautionary note, graphic organizers are time-consuming and therefore should not be used excessively because they will lead to boredom and also will negate instructional time that should be used for other valuable activities. A practical guide to follow is to use a variety of graphic organizers and to connect them to **challenging vocabulary and concepts that are essential for comprehension of content**. Consider examples of graphic organizers in Figures 3.1–3.9 that may be completed individually or collaboratively.

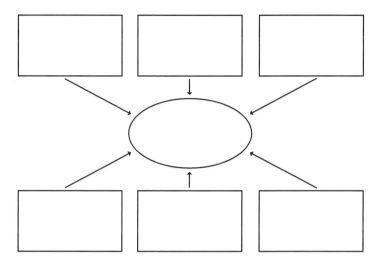

Figure 3.1 Concept Map

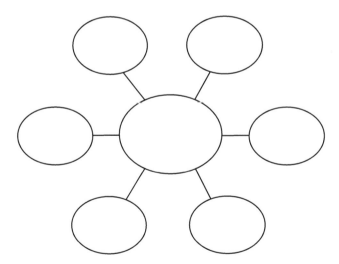

Figure 3.2 Semantic Map

28 ◆ Promoting Critical Thinking

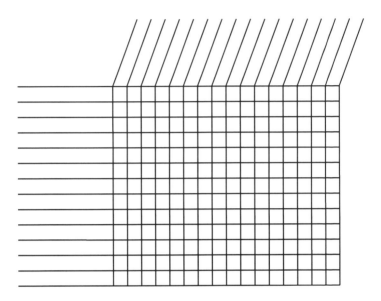

Figure 3.3 Semantic Feature Analysis Grid

K-W-L-Y

K̲NOW	W̲ANT to KNOW	L̲EARNED	Y̲ET to LEARN

Figure 3.4 K-W-L-Y

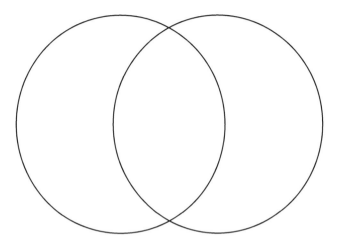

Figure 3.5 Venn Diagram

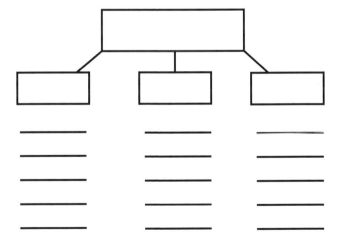

Figure 3.6 Structured (Hierarchy) Overview

30 ◆ Promoting Critical Thinking

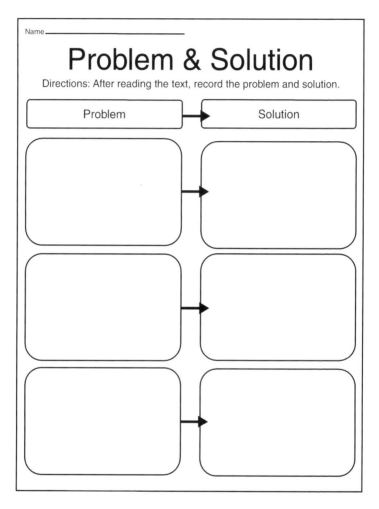

Figure 3.7 Problem and Solution Map

Promoting Critical Thinking ♦ 31

Anticipation Guide

Statement	Agree/Disagree	I was Right? Wrong? Why?

Figure 3.8 Anticipation Guide

Causes and Effects

Causes	Effects

Figure 3.9 Causes and Effects

4
Application and Transfer of Learning

The suggestions in this book reflect both explicit and student-centered considerations, and they support students' efforts to gain insights about varied aspects of political rhetoric. As students apply critical-thinking skills and strategies during thoughtful and thought-provoking content assignments, their efforts can result in the desired goal of achieving transfer of learning. This hard work is more productive than isolated, literal-level assignments that often result in boredom, fragmented learning outcomes, and minimal transfer value. Consider the following challenging assignments:

Channel-Surfing

One way of promoting higher interactive thinking with transfer value is to encourage students to work as productive teams, with a sense of belonging, as they spend time:

> channel-surfing news programs and then report and discuss over the next several days on these questions: What stories were being reported on by various stations? What spin was placed on the same story as reported by different news services? What, if any, primary sources were used or quoted in the stories? (Do they know what a primary source is?) The discussion might then move to commentary and reporting around the same or similar stories that they may have seen in newspapers and magazines or on social media. Special attention should be paid to the validation of Internet sources in general. Further discussion could focus on where and how factual information can be obtained and what role responsible journalists should play in fact-checking stories (Noddings & Brooks, 2017, pp. 94–95).

ThinkCERCA Platform

A complementary approach to applying critical thinking was carried out at Lodi High School in Lodi, Wisconsin (Cramer &

Hubers, 2016). The project focused on political ads and the extensive information—and misinformation—that students encounter often. The intent of the project was to nurture students' critical thinking about the political process in a nonpartisan and unbiased way, "giving them the power to sift through the reams of information we're inundated with on a daily basis and decide what to trust and what to be skeptical about—and how to go about making those determinations." The tool to teach about politics was ThinkCERCA, which is a literacy platform for creating lessons on current events and other topics that motivate critical thinking and argumentative writing. For the 2016 presidential election, ThinkCERCA created a central hub, which provided pertinent resources and writing prompts. Students became immersed in a substantial amount of information from which to choose, and they focused in depth on many aspects of the election process. Then, they engaged in a final project that involved "close reads" of political advertisements, during which they also learned about multiple topics. These topics included the U.S. election process, election speak, political platforms, political ideologies, political information sources, and different political races. Students also had opportunities to assess their understanding of the political gamut and to investigate limited sources of political information. To support productive outcomes of the project, students became immersed in group discussions and individual writing, and they were encouraged to think about the following critical questions for their politics-based assignment: "Where am I getting my information about candidates that run for office? How does this affect my knowledge base? And how do I determine what are conservative and liberal ideologies of candidates/major political parties?" Students watched political ads multiple times and used them and what they learned in class to gain evidence that supported their claims. Then, they wrote an argumentative paper in the ThinkCERCA platform "using the CERCA Framework as their guide. The

CERCA Framework, a cornerstone of the tool, emphasizes Claims, Evidence, Reasoning, Counterarguments, and Audience-appropriate language to create strong and well-reasoned arguments." Overall, Cramer and Hubers's (2016) comprehensive project on critical thinking is a useful example that can be adapted to other extended learning contexts.

Productive Group Work: 1935 Social Security Act

Immersing students in a project related to the 1935 Social Security Act further supports the value of applying and transferring higher interactive thinking skills (HITS) to novel settings. When educators adapt some of Vaca, Lapp, and Fisher's (2011) principles for successful group work, they become an important factor in promoting a community of learners who engage in pertinent interactions with one another.

> The first, and most obvious, characteristic of successful group work is to design tasks that cause students to talk with one another, to hear how their peers approach the content and then to be able to compare this with their own approach. Second, the task must provide a stimulus question or problem that causes students to cooperate as they formulate, share, and compare ideas with one another. Finally, all tasks should be broad enough to involve both individual and group accountability (pp. 372–373).

Vaca, Lapp, and Fisher applied these principles to productive group work involving U.S. history instruction. Small heterogeneous groups of students were to determine the benefits of the 1935 Social Security Act and the U.S. government's use of posters to communicate those benefits to the American people. Each group received a packet, which included five tasks to be completed. Task 1 highlighted preparation for group work (i.e., students were given guidelines for analyzing, discussing, and responding to U.S. government posters to promote the Social Security Act's passage). Task 2 supported collaborative efforts (i.e., after analyzing the posters, group members shared and recorded classmates' reflections). Task 3 invited critical analysis (i.e., students supported the Social Security Act by creating present-day posters that made connections to current issues and to today's diverse society). Task 4 assessed group performance (i.e., group members presented a comprehensive collection of posters that represented social diversity, and they reflected on the messages of each poster and determined each poster's appeal to the unemployed, widowed women, and retirement-age citizens). Task 5 assessed individual performance (i.e., students wrote individual responses to thoughtful prompts as a way of showing their understanding of the Social Security Act's intent).

Although these efforts were primarily intended to improve productivity in group work, they also supported aspects of part-whole, multimodal learning by encouraging students to analyze and visually divide government posters into four sections (parts) as a way of interpreting the government's purpose for producing the posters (whole). Students also reflected on this experience and then created their own present-day posters that provided support for the Social Security Act. Examining the details of government posters helped group members to understand their intended message and, in turn, to generate original posters. Teachers can also encourage another dimension of this process by guiding students to create other venues, such as dressing in costumes and pantomiming varied roles that support different views of the Social Security Act. For example, they can incorporate instrumental music, dance, song, or other physical manifestations, as they pantomime and express their 1935 or present-day perspectives on Social Security. Additional information on productive group work, differentiated small-group instruction, and multimodal perspectives can be found, respectively, in Frey, Fisher, and Everlove (2009); Lapp, Fisher, and Wolsey (2009); and Sanacore and Piro (2014).

Sports and Society Class

Another innovative example of applying critical thinking was promoted in Toni West's (2019) Sports and Society class at Moreau Catholic High School in Hayward, California. She refocused this elective class so that it was better aligned to the school's mission, part of which states, "We are committed to preparing our students through academic, social and spiritual learning experiences that form and transform them into responsible citizens of our global community." Realizing that her students loved sports, West channeled their passion to enact change. She created a learning environment that increased students' awareness of what was important to them, how to articulate their points of view, and how to engage in related research. The emphasis of the course was to confront issues that shape society. To accomplish these and other course priorities, West and her students established criteria for critical thinking, communication, and respectful dialogue. "After all, in order to practice open-mindedness, students need to be able to speak, debate, and disagree in such a way that no one feels intimidated about expressing opinions." With these norms established, students were initially challenged to determine their own ability to think critically as they responded to statements like:

1. I do not simply accept conclusions; I evaluate and critique the underlying reasons.
2. I recognize irrelevant facts and false assumptions, and I discount them.
3. I am able to consider the strengths and weaknesses of my own point of view and that of opposing positions.

This reflection set the stage for tackling challenging social issues that students were passionately interested in solving.

After learning about facts and contexts of varied problems, students viewed related documentaries and also engaged in current events discussions. From these experiences, students learned about a variety of issues, including homeless high school athletes from different countries who were selected to compete in the Homeless World Cup. As the documentaries increased their awareness of important issues—some political and economic—students held debates that highlighted such topics as male and female athletes receiving unequal pay, colleges violating NCAA eligibility rules for student athletes, and a female basketball player accusing a football player of raping her at a party. In discussing the issue of rape, students were organized in groups and assigned different roles, including athletic director, women's basketball coach, head football coach, college president, and booster club president. In each group, they researched their job title and how they may respond in a scenario. Specifically, in those challenging roles, "students had to think about how they might act differently to protect their jobs or protect those who they are supposed to protect. This exercise required them to research actual cases and statistics concerning rape on campus."

Pairing of Easy and Challenging Texts

Another instructional strategy for applying and transferring HITS to content is to engage students in the pairing of easy and challenging literature (Palumbo & Sanacore, 2013). The fact that some students struggle with reading should not deny them the opportunity to become immersed in serious thought and related critical thinking. These individuals benefit initially from reading, discussing, and writing about comparable subject matter in young adult (YA) literature, which is often easier for them to read and relate to than more advanced books. Not surprisingly, many YA books contain serious subject matter about themes that highlight friendship and love, social and emotional issues, good and evil, race and police relations, gun violence and gun control, grief and coping, and other areas that are important to people's lives. For struggling or reluctant readers, the YA literature experience will suffice at this time in their literacy development. For others, however, exposure to YA books will motivate and prepare them to better understand and appreciate similar subject matter in more challenging literature.

Many sources are available for pairing the themes and concepts of YA literature with more challenging versions, and a sampling is included here:

- Kate Bolick, Jenny Zhang, Carmen Maria Machado, and Jane Smiley's *March Sisters* **WITH** Louisa May Alcott's *Little Women*
- Sharon Draper's *Romiette and Julio* and Arthur Laurents' *West Side Story* **WITH** William Shakespeare's *Romeo and Juliet*
- Lois Duncan's *Killing Mr. Griffin* and Todd Strasser's *The Wave* **WITH** William Golding's *Lord of the Flies*
- Robert Cormier's *The Chocolate War* and Orson Scott Card's *Ender's Game* **WITH** George Orwell's *1984*
- Chris Crutcher's *Ironman* and Chris Lynch's *Iceman* **WITH** J.D. Salinger's *Catcher in the Rye*
- Bette Green's *Summer of My German Soldier* and Lois Lowry's *Number the Stars* **WITH** Anne Frank's *Diary of a Young Girl*
- S.E. Hinton's *The Outsiders* and Rodman Philbrick's *Freak the Mighty* **WITH** John Steinbeck's *Of Mice and Men*
- Margo Livesey's *The Flight of Gemma Hardy* **WITH** Charlotte Brontë's *Jane Eyre*
- Priya Parmar's *Vanessa and Her Sister* **WITH** Virginia Woolf's *To the Lighthouse*
- Jerry Spinelli's *Maniac Magee* **WITH** Mark Twain's *Adventures of Tom Sawyer*
- Donna Tartt's *The Goldfinch* **WITH** Charles Dickens' *Great Expectations*

- Mildred Taylor's *Roll of Thunder, Hear My Cry* and Harper Lee and Kerry Madden's *Up Close* **WITH** Harper Lee's *To kill a Mockingbird*

Middle-level learners are able to make a transition from YA books to challenging versions when teachers provide support, including the aid of graphic organizers that were discussed earlier. One type of commonly used graphic organizer, the Venn diagram, offers students a way to engage in the higher-level thinking skills of comparing and contrasting important elements of books. According to Yopp and Yopp (2006):

> Venn diagrams provide graphic representations, in the form of overlapping circles, of features that are unique and common to selected topics. The readers draw two or more overlapping circles and label each circle. Where the circles overlap, features common to the topics are listed, and where they do not overlap, features unique to each topic are recorded (p. 112).

Appropriate use of Venn diagrams and other graphic organizers can support students' success as they make transitions from YA literature to more challenging text, especially when teachers guide students to engage in small-group conversations about important text elements. Middle-level and secondary-level learners, including those who struggle with reading and writing, use the information learned in this way to write thoughtful, reflective reviews of the books they compared and contrasted. For a comprehensive review of the professional literature, with related implications for instruction, see Miller's (2017) dissertation titled *Pairing Young Adult and Classic Literature in the High School English Curriculum*.

Pairing of Traditional Books, Graphic Books, and Film Versions

When students read, enjoy, and talk about interesting books, they appreciate opportunities to view movie versions, either in school or at home. Comparing and contrasting traditional print and film adaptations bring deeper meaning to class discussions, writing assignments, and small-group projects. Teachers are encouraged to enrich school curricula with print and media sources and to guide students to enjoy and respect them as supportive partners for interpreting and appreciating related concepts and themes.

Graphic novels and graphic nonfiction books are also important resources that can help students to extend their understanding of the world via multimodal contexts. Graphic literature is based in the comics genre (Marlatt & Dallacqua, 2019) and can be an empowering source of motivation for applying HITS across the curriculum. As students become immersed in this type of content area instruction, they experience another dimension of learning that can have a profound impact on their literacy growth. For example, teachers can provide experiences that complement traditional print by increasing students' awareness of speech and thought balloons, frames, panels, line, color, shading, and other graphic elements. As students gain insights about the comic format, they develop an appreciation for the ways in which the comic genre supports the telling of a sequential story with creative images that scaffold meaning making.

Both graphic novels and nonfiction graphic books are excellent resources that support content area learning, and Don Brown's nonfiction comic *Drowned City: Hurricane Katrina and New Orleans* provides an optimal context for emphasizing literacy across the curriculum. This book is visually compelling and uses line, shading, and color to create foreshadowing and mood (Marlatt & Dallacqua, 2019). When compared with multiple versions of Hurricane Katrina—films, documentaries, YouTube videos, books, and other texts—students are challenged to think critically as they ask questions and differentiate factual content from inaccurate news.

What follows is a sampling of traditional literature and adaptations in graphic book form. These and other works of literature have also been produced as films and videos.

- *Anne Frank: Diary of a Young Girl* **AND** *Anne Frank's Diary: The Graphic Adaptation*
- *The Giver* **AND** *The Giver: The Graphic Novel*
- *The Good Earth* **AND** *The Good Earth: Graphic Adaptation*
- *The Great Gatsby* **AND** *The Great Gatsby: The Graphic Novel*
- *Hamlet, Julius Caesar, Macbeth, A Midsummer Night's Dream,* and *Romeo and Juliet* **AND** *Graphic Shakespeare: Romeo and Juliet, Julius Caesar, Hamlet, Macbeth, and A Midsummer Night's Dream*
- *Les Miserables* **AND** *Les Miserables: A Graphic Novel*
- *Moby Dick* **AND** *Moby Dick: The Graphic Novel*
- *To Kill a Mockingbird* **AND** *To Kill a Mockingbird: A Graphic Novel*
- *The Witches* **AND** *The Witches: The Graphic Novel*
- *A Wrinkle in Time* **AND** *A Wrinkle in Time: The Graphic Novel*
- The fable or fairy tale *The Three Little Pigs* **AND** *The Three Little Pigs: The Graphic Novel* **AND** *The True Story of the 3 Little Pigs*

For additional sources, visit https://www.google.com/search?source = univ&tbm = isch&q = Graphic + novel + adaptations + of + classic + literature & sa = X & ved = 2ahUKEwj9h5S-lZftAhVVSTABHd_pCBQQ420oA3oECAMQCg &biw = 1051 & bih = 461 https://www.google.com/search?source = univ & tbm = isch & q = Graphic + novel + adaptations + of + classic + literature & sa = X & ved = 2ahUKEwj9h5SlZftAhVVSTABHd_pCBQQ420oA3oECAMQCg&biw = 1051 & bih = 461.

Among the best ways to connect critical thinking and graphic literature are to demonstrate respect for graphic books as legitimate instructional resources and to ask serious questions during classroom discussions. Stearns (2020) suggests modifying questions to accommodate students' interests and abilities but remaining pertinent to the specific graphic texts that students are studying. The following questions have been adapted and might be helpful as teachers engage students in interactive discussions about characters and plot.

Character questions include:

- After describing the main and supporting characters of the graphic book, what lead to your interpretation of the characters' personality traits?
- Which characters are most and least convincing to you, and why?
- Is the body language of the characters relevant to their personalities, and if so, to what extent?
- Do the characters change throughout the print and cartoon text? How does the author create these changes, and why (or why not) do you consider these changes to be realistic?
- If you only read the print text or only read the illustration text, describe how the characters would seem different. As the characters are developed, how do these elements of traditional and visual text work together?

Plot questions include:

- Using examples from the graphic book, describe why or why not the plot is convincing, realistic, and meaningful.
- Do the comic images and traditional print work

together seamlessly? If the book did not provide graphic text, how would you have interpreted it differently?
- Describe the major problems in the plot, and indicate to what degree the plot is driven by these problems.
- Is the book organized around one major plot or varied subplots? How do you feel about the structure of the plot?
- Explain how the setting contributes to the plot. If the same or similar plot occurred in a different time and place, how would the resolutions or outcomes be different?
- Think about working with a partner and creating a story or nonfiction piece that connects both print and graphic text. Feel free to enhance the meaning and enjoyment of your work by combining traditional print, speech and thought balloons, frames, panels, line, color, shading, and other graphic elements.

Not surprisingly, there are many ways of learning and knowing, and students are more likely to embrace the classroom culture when it affords opportunities to demonstrate their strengths and interests in a variety and diversity of texts, including traditional books, graphic books, film versions, and other multimodal forms.

Inferences and Children's Literature

Teachers are sometimes anxious about nurturing young children's growth and development in critical thinking. They understandably are concerned about providing developmentally appropriate instruction that does not frustrate children's learning capacity. When teachers review related research and professional literature, as well as engage in reflection through practical experience, they come to realize that young children are interested in and capable of embracing the challenges of HITS.

While focusing on children's literature as an impetus for inferential discussions, Kelly and Moses (2018) provided a pertinent review of studies that support the value of inferencing and meaning making for young children. From their review of the research literature, Kelly and Moses' study was based on several assumptions:

> that inferencing is a critical comprehension skill that can be taught, that discussions about children's literature provide effective contexts for inferencing instruction, and that teachers should teach inferencing to primary students still learning to decode (p. 22).

The first-grade children selected for this study were from a range of socioeconomic, cultural, and linguistic backgrounds. An interesting and pragmatic part of the study highlighted three types of children's books that promote inferential thinking and flexible discussion groups, with transcripts that focused on how the books facilitated inference making. As the children were immersed in quality literature with rich typography, illustrations, and design elements, they benefited from these multimodal connections to *ambiguous*, *didactic*, and *fractured* texts. Ambiguous books intentionally do not provide some details, which motivate young readers to fill these narrative gaps with inference making. Didactic books encourage children to infer the authors' and illustrators' messages (a bit of a theme or moral of stories), which often involve informing or instructing young readers. Fractured fairy tales motivate children to infer the trustworthiness of the narrators.

A sampling of the types of books includes:

- ♦ Ambiguous texts, such as Jon Klassen's *This Is Not My*

Hat, Emily Gravett's *Wolves*, and Chris Raschka's *Yo! Yes*
- Didactic texts, such as Mayra Lazara Dole's *Drum, Chavi, Drum!/¡Toca, Chavi, Toca!*, Steve Antony's *Please, Mr. Panda/Por Favor, Sr. Panda*, and Miriam B. Schiffer's *Stella Brings the Family*
- Fractured fairy tales, such as Tomie dePaola's *Adelita: A Mexican Cinderella Story*, Jon Scieszka's *The True Story of the Three Little Pigs*, and Mo Willems's *Goldilocks and the Three Dinosaurs*.

This study provided further support for engaging young children in profound talk about quality literature, and an important source of support was the inclusion of multimodal perspectives. When primary school teachers foster inferential discussions of children's books, they set a positive foundation for helping young children to develop confidence and competence with inferencing and other critical thinking skills.

Painting Writing, Writing Painting

Supporting more multimodal connections to young children's reading and writing is beneficial for their growth and development in HITS because it values different modes to meaning as it respects individual feelings, interests, strengths, and learning needs. Regrettably, school administrators and classroom teachers are under incredible stress to have students achieve high results on norm-referenced and standards-oriented exams. These national and state tests typically emphasize traditional print with minimal opportunities for students to respond to other types of text, including artists' illustrations. Traditional print still dominates test items and related questions, which encourage the use of teaching strategies and instructional resources that are matched with the goals and objectives of the tests. With such a limited view of literacy assessment and instruction, these tests reinforce the age-old adage, "What doesn't get tested, doesn't get taught."

What is needed is a greater emphasis on valuing and respecting traditional print, story illustrations, and other multimodal texts as equitable partners that promote meaning making. Fortunately, researchers and practitioners are supporting efforts to empower young children to compose in art and written language. In the Martens et al. (2018) study, kindergarten and first-grade children were afforded opportunities to "paint writing and write painting." As readers, writers, and artists, the children were grounded in the semantic/pragmatic, syntactic, and graphophonic cuing systems. This foundation increased an awareness of elements of art, such as color, form, line, shape, space, and texture. Mindfulness of the principles of design were also an important part of the classroom culture, and they included balance, contrast, emphasis, harmony, movement, and variety. While the children became immersed in discussions of selected picture books with art concepts, they progressed in their understanding of *line* and *space* as elements of art and of *contrast* as a principle of design. Through their engagement in art and writing, they became increasingly creative as they developed their seeing, thinking, and problem solving. These personal and creative outcomes were accomplished in several ways:

> First, students imaginatively, creatively, and eagerly told their stories in their own voices … Second, the students' stories evidenced their thinking, reasoning, decision-making, and ability to see … Third, to compose, students seamlessly wove together meanings they represented in different symbolic systems (Martens et al., 2018, p. 677).

As young children's learning capacity is enhanced and appreciated, they can more easily connect their growing creativity and critical thinking insights to other venues.

Reflective Practice and Service Learning

At West Chester University's Center for Civic Engagement and Social Impact (CCESI, 2020), students can engage in reflection as an important part of service learning. Through the process of guiding and structuring students' reflective process, teachers are able to help students integrate their community experiences with classroom theories, thereby facilitating their efforts to gain additional insights about critical thinking with transfer value. This learning context affords opportunities to respond to civic experiences with a critical framework for challenging stereotypes, correcting assumptions, feeling personal growth, developing citizenship skills, and sharing feelings and reactions with peers. Although this perspective is intended for mature students, it can be applied in developmentally appropriate ways to learners of all ages and grade levels.

Because quality reflection is a vitally important part of students' experiences, it should be intentional, well organized, and ongoing, and it should occur before, during, and after students' service experiences (CCESI, 2020; see also Eyler, Giles, & Schmiede, 1996). The following are examples and adaptations of reflection assignments that have transfer value:

- Students write journal entries, engage in classroom discussions, and post online blogs, all of which are meaningful responses to teachers' analytical questions about service learning.
- Students demonstrate their community-based experience with multimodal texts, including print, digital, video, photography, drawing, painting, documentary, music, and choreography.
- Students choose a theory or idea discussed in class and apply it analytically to their service experience.
- Students create a visual map that connects their

service-learning experience to bigger issues at the state, national, and international levels.
♦ Students address issues that are important to the community organizations in which they are working by writing an individual or group letter to the media and to government officials.
♦ Students locate and share stories, articles, and songs that connect with their service experience.

These and other activities support the value of reflection based on students' lived-through experiences, and they are especially beneficial for learners' growth and development when they have been analyzed, synthesized, applied, and evaluated with the guidance of moral criticism (Noddings & Brooks, 2017).

Immigrants, Jobs, and Crime

Guidance in moral criticism is certainly needed when students are engaged in potentially controversial topics, and issues related to immigrants have been the "heated" focus of politicians and the media during the past several decades. Regrettably, some politicians and media sources have continued to articulate arguments about immigrants, blaming them for imposing economic hardships on middle-class Americans. To determine if these arguments are based in fiction or nonfiction, students need to become immersed in research, discussions, and collaborative projects with the intent of determining the truth. Guiding questions might include: Are the wages of low-skilled immigrants compared to wages of low-skilled Americans without a high school diploma or to middle-class Americans? What are the job categories that will show the greatest growth in the next ten years, and what percentage of these jobs will require no formal credentials? What is the expected increase of these unskilled jobs during the next ten years? Does immigration make the American population wealthier or poorer? How much money do immigrants contribute to the American tax base? What data have you found that support your conclusions? What other questions do you want to ask about immigrants and jobs?

Regrettably, some politicians, media sources, parents, and others also argue that immigrants are responsible for excessive crime in the United States. To determine if these claims have merit, guiding questions might include: Are immigrants less likely or more likely to commit crimes than native-born Americans? Are immigrant men less likely or more likely to be incarcerated compared to their native-born counterparts? What percentage of immigrants are inmates in state and federal prisons? What data have you found that support your conclusions? What other questions do you want to ask about immigrants and crime?

Compounding issues related to immigrants are claims about the Deferred Action on Childhood Arrivals (DACA), which affects nearly 800,000 young immigrants (often referred to as "Dreamers"). These immigrants were given a reprieve from deportation and were afforded the opportunity to work legally in the United States. Some politicians and media sources made claims about the high cost of supporting immigrants and DACA. To determine the efficacy of these claims, guiding questions might include: If DACA were repealed, would fiscal costs be imposed on the federal government and the economy? If so, what would be the aggregate cost to the economy and the cost to the government? Do the Dreamers do well in school and, consequently, in the job market after they complete school? Do undocumented immigrants provide substantial tax contributions? If so, then collectively, what are their estimated annual contributions in personal income taxes, property taxes, and local taxes? What data have you found to support your conclusions? What other questions do you want to ask about immigrants and DACA?

Guiding students to engage in research, discussions, and collaborative projects concerning this potentially controversial topic will help them to separate facts from "fictions." This outcome, however, will not come easily. Especially needed is a caring teacher who supports students' efforts to demonstrate civility as they agree and disagree on a number of related issues. During these "active" discussions, students are challenged to consider how their positionality affects their epistemology—that is, how one's stance in relation to the social and political context biases one's ability to distinguish justified beliefs from opinions (Takacs, 2003). Meanwhile, the teacher is also challenged to not sway students, directly or subtly, to her or his position.

Independent Reading, Vocabulary Development, and Comprehension

All of the previous activities in this booklet either directly or indirectly support the value and use of vocabulary in meaningful contexts. There are a number of reasons for increasing students' vocabulary:

1. Research supports the positive correlations and relationships between vocabulary knowledge and comprehension ability (Anderson & Freebody, 1981; Elleman, Lindo, Morphy, & Compton, 2009; Kameli, & Baki, 2013; Nagy & Scott, 2000).
2. As a group, disadvantaged learners begin school aware of only half the words that advantaged children know (Hart & Risley, 1995).
3. Students' reading fluency, comprehension, and vocabulary increase substantially when students engage in wide and varied reading of a volume of material in school and at home (Allington, 1977; Sanacore, 2010). If vocabulary is taught directly or explicitly, students will learn an estimated 400 words a year (Beck, McKeown, & Kucan, 2002), which are inadequate for reading

comprehension requirements across the curriculum and through the grades. Students need to learn several thousand words each year to deal successfully with curricular expectations, and one of the more practical and effective ways of nurturing extensive vocabulary growth is to give students opportunities to engage in actual reading of a volume of different types of text.
4. Learners with extensive word knowledge are more apt to achieve academic success because they are able to interpret new ideas and concepts more readily than learners with limited vocabulary knowledge (Sedita, 2005).
5. As students increase their vocabulary and comprehension, they bring more quality and quantity of prior knowledge to the critical thinking process.

Because guided independent reading can increase vocabulary development, comprehension ability, and HITS, students benefit substantially from a comprehensive support system that consists of a classroom resource center, effective read-alouds, and time to read in school and at home.

A classroom resource center should include a wide variety of materials that accommodate students' interests and learning levels and also afford opportunities to become immersed in a diversity of multimodal experiences. A comprehensive and balanced collection includes the following resources, adapted and expanded from Sanacore (2006):

- updated informational text
- narrative materials, including animated narratives
- poetry anthologies, including performance poetry
- screen-based or digital texts
- e-books
- picture or illustrated books, including informational, narrative, and poetic
- biographies
- autobiographies

- science information books
- historical fiction
- how-to-books
- comics
- graphic novels and graphic nonfiction books
- art
- dance, including magnificent examples of "Chinese Dance" and other culturally based choreography shown in documentaries, YouTube videos, Vimeo productions, and films
- drawing
- portraiture
- photography
- claymation
- music
- multicultural materials, including informational, narrative, and poetic
- bibliotherapeutic stories and information sources
- materials and projects written and illustrated by children
- films, documentaries, and YouTube videos
- multimedia software and hardware
- adaptive software and hardware
- audio books
- large-print books
- magazines
- newspapers
- pamphlets

Although it takes time and energy to build an effective classroom resource center, these and other resources are important for encouraging students to become independent readers of a wide variety of text and, simultaneously, to enjoy these meaningful contexts as vehicles for making connections between vocabulary and higher-level comprehension skills.

Students are more apt to make these connections when teachers demonstrate their value with effective read-alouds that support thematic learning. For example, when addressing an instructional theme, such as "Is War Ever Justified?" the teacher can read aloud sources with different text types that speak to the theme from different (pro and con) perspectives. On Monday, the teacher might share parts of narrative stories; on Tuesday, the teacher might read aloud sections of informational books; and on Wednesday, the teacher might share several poems. Before, during, and after each read-aloud, the teacher encourages students to interact and transact with the text as students make predictions, confirm or disconfirm their predictions, respond personally and critically to the content, verify personal responses, and engage in comparative analyses of how different text structures convey meaning. In both the read-alouds and related discussions, the teacher must not bias students, either directly or subtly, with his or her position concerning the theme "Is War Ever Justified?" or other subject area concepts that are potentially controversial.

Read-alouds and class discussions are thoughtful ways of enhancing vocabulary knowledge and comprehension skills via interesting and meaningful resources. These experiences are especially beneficial when students have opportunities to choose books from the classroom resource center and to read them for pleasure. This requires allotting time for browsing, selecting, and reading materials. According to Allington (2006), elementary school children should be engaged in actual in-school reading for ninety minutes a day. This amount of reading time is beneficial for students, but it is difficult to schedule in middle schools and high schools because forty-minute instructional periods typically dominate most secondary school schedules. If block scheduling has been implemented (i.e., back-to-back, eighty-minute periods), then independent reading could be extended for longer sessions (Sanacore & Palumbo, 2010).

Considering the forty-minute limitation in most secondary schools, the class schedule in Figure 4.1 is an ambitious attempt to support independent reading across the curriculum by including substantial time to read in class. Teachers and administrators are welcome to adapt this model to their students' strengths, needs, and interests. Note that each ten-week progress period provides five weeks for independent reading and five weeks for traditional curricular activities (TCA), such as direct instruction and student-centered engagement in English language arts, social studies, science, and mathematics. Teachers can reverse the time allotment to reflect TCA for the first five weeks and independent reading for the last five weeks of each progress period. Time has not been allotted for independent reading in art, music, physical education, and other special area classes because they typically meet less often during the school year, and teachers might have less time to cover required content. Students in special area classes, however, benefit from opportunities to interpret and appreciate text in paintings, musical compositions, spatial movements, and other meaningful contexts. To make this ambitious model a success, flexibility is necessary. For example, based on curricular requirements, some of the ten-week progress periods of the school year might allot three or four weeks or six

	First 10-Week Progress Period	Second 10-Week Progress Period	Third 10-Week Progress Period	Fourth 10-Week Progress Period
ELA	IR...TCA			
Social Studies		IR...TCA		
Science			IR...TCA	
Mathematics				IR...TCA

Figure 4.1 Ambitious Model of Secondary School Students' Yearlong Schedule That Includes Independent Reading

or seven weeks for independent reading. Furthermore, some schools use a tri-semester schedule, so different time allotments for independent reading are probably needed. The important point here is to consider engagement in actual reading as an essential priority because it not only supports the lifetime reading/literacy habit but also builds subject knowledge that is useful for applying HITS. These are big-picture considerations.

Regardless of the scheduling process, students need opportunities to become immersed in narrative, informational, poetic, and other multimodal texts. These experiences will help students to engage in thoughtful and thought-provoking discussions and activities across the curriculum and to build background knowledge for thinking critically. For example, in a social studies unit, students can develop a better understanding of the past and how it can create a better future. Students can critically analyze resources that highlight such topics as how historical roots connect to the present and future, how geographic perspectives relate to diverse cultures, how different cultures enrich one another, how climate change affects the planet, and how war impacts different societies. From these subject-based topics, students can gain important insights about interdisciplinary concepts that can be applied to art, music, science, mathematics, English language arts, and other curricular areas. To illustrate, if we focus on how climate change affects the planet, our community of learners can engage in activities and small-group projects that explore and analyze how learning across the curriculum supports beautiful and meaningful connections that help everyone to better understand climate change (Brookshire, 2019). *Climate Quest*, for example, is a game created by climate scientist Dargan Frierson. *A painted sign*, created by Xavier Cortada, is a marker that home owners can plant in their yard that demonstrates how high the sea would have to rise to flood the home (5 feet, or 1.5 meters). *A Song of Our Warming Planet is* a musical piece that was inspired by Daniel Crawford's profound interest in climate data. Michele

Banks's artistic piece, the *Marriage of Ice and Carbon, the Arctic Bride*, highlights a typical white wedding dress that symbolizes the Arctic's ice. As the climate warms, however, the frosty Arctic melts, and the wedding dress dissolves into a weedy mass. According to Banks, "It doesn't give you a feeling of growth. It's that icky dull brown and green that you see when the snow melts … That's a lot of what's up in the Arctic right now. It's not a happy green." Choreographer Diana Movius's glacial dance, titled *Glacial: Multimedia Climate Change Ballet*, is a Vimeo production. It symbolizes movement as dancers perform in front of drifting ice images, with their bodies showing a process called calving, or how glaciers separate from ice sheets and melt into the sea.

These and other interdisciplinary explorations of climate change can be further supported with related websites and guiding questions, which enhance rich conversations and writing assignments. For example, Murray-Everett and Coffield (2020) suggest the following websites to locate webpages, articles, and other sources:

- www.nasa.gov
- www.climaterealityproject.org
- www.carbonfootprint.com

Because all people, websites, and texts are not neutral (Kelly, Laminack, & Gould, 2020; Laminack & Kelly, 2019), teachers and students are encouraged to pursue a variety of informational sources with different perspectives. Students can use this information as they respond to pertinent questions, adapted here:

- How do scientists explain the effects of climate change on weather patterns (hurricanes, wildfires, early snowfalls, droughts, and ice fields melting)?
- Is it important for the United States to become "carbon neutral" by 2050? Why or why not? Is it possible or

probable for the United States to become "carbon neutral" by 2050? Why or why not?
♦ Should "climate change" be a top concern for elected officials? Why or why not? (Murray-Everett & Coffield, 2020, p. 6).

These are important academic pursuits that afford opportunities for learning about the many interdisciplinary dimensions of an instructional theme or unit. This interesting, meaningful context also provides an open-minded atmosphere for connecting, extending, and applying vocabulary and comprehension and for building a foundation in curricular accomplishment and lifetime learning (Sanacore & Palumbo, 2010).

When teachers use independent reading to promote vocabulary development and reading comprehension with different types of text—for example, art, music, photography, dance, print—this student-centered approach should not negate the value of using teacher-directed methodologies that provide additional support. Such support is especially needed for "essential" vocabulary, which helps students to grasp the meaning of domain-specific words for interpreting text. In social studies, for example, teachers can use maps or concept-of-definition maps (Sanacore & Palumbo, 2010; Schwartz, 1998; Schwartz & Raphael, 1985). As students discuss a specific term like *compromises*, they are asked to consider its category (What is it?), properties (What is it like?), and illustrations (What are some examples of this term?). When the class discussion is connected to a concept-of-definition map about compromises in American History, thoughts can be directed toward the development of a map that might include a category (promise), properties (mutual concessions), and examples (Missouri Compromise or Compromise of 1877). Students can then synthesize this information on the map to write a definition of the term *compromise*. Beyond the concept-of-definition map, teachers have options of incorporating Six Steps to Effective Vocabulary Instruction (Marzano, 2004), the Frayer Model (Frayer, Frederick, & Klausmeier, 1969; Buehl, 2014), and other explicit instructional approaches (NBSS, n.d.). That said, teacher-directed instruction is more likely to support students' vocabulary development and reading comprehension when the concepts that are studied come from meaningful contexts, are discussed and elaborated in depth, and result in transfer of learning to other reading and writing activities that reinforce the meaning of comparable concepts. This sends a positive message to students that the purpose of expanding their vocabulary is to improve their understanding and use of a diversity of text.

As educators support independent reading, vocabulary development, and reading comprehension, they will witness a lessening of the insidious problem of aliteracy that affects many Americans who can read but choose not to read. Estimating the percentage of aliterates, however, is both nonproductive and inaccurate because some estimates highlight only those who don't read traditional print and exclude those who read digital and other types of multimodal texts. Educators are encouraged to take the road less traveled by defining text broadly and by giving students opportunities to choose, read, and appreciate a diversity of text that is personally interesting and meaningful. Such a broad-based culture of literacy can have positive transfer value to students' lifetime love of learning.

Creativity and Problem Solving

Although aspects of creativity have not been directly addressed in this book, solving complex problems in novel ways has often been implicitly connected to creative thinking. When learners experience new situations and tasks, they often use creative thinking (Sternberg, 2005). It is essential, however, that learners engage in reflective judgment when the new situations and tasks require careful consideration, such as individuals' "purposeful, self-regulated consideration and understanding of the nature, limits, and certainty of knowing; how this can affect how they defend their judgments and reasoning in context; and acknowledgement that their views might be falsified by additional evidence obtained at a later time" (Dwyer, 2018; see also Dwyer, 2017; King & Kitchener, 1994).

John Paul II (1979) recognized the spiritual and earthly value of creativity by noting that humans have exceptional capacities that can bring about creative restlessness, culminating in what is most deeply human: hunger for freedom, nostalgia for the beautiful, the insatiable need for the good, the voice of conscience, and the search for truth. At the very least, creative thinking and problem solving involve having the courage to leave one's comfort zone and to delve into the unknown. Fourteen-year-old student and writer Line Dalile (2012) has demonstrated the courage to speak out: "Creativity isn't a test to take, a skill to learn, or a program to develop. Creativity is seeing things in new ways, breaking barriers that stood in front of you for some time ... I want to imagine, to create, to be the best I can possibly be. I never want to be a robot."

When teachers motivate students to articulate a strong voice, they also recognize students' need for space to grow and develop as independent, creative problem solvers. An inclusive approach to supporting this perspective is design thinking, which is a framework, mindset, and strategy for collaborating, learning, problem solving, and building creative confidence. Design thinking provides opportunities "for observing and understanding the challenges people experience, defining and positioning those challenges as design opportunities, and generating, refining, and testing possible solutions. As a group of mindsets, design thinking encourages empathy, collaboration, communication, and experimentation. Design thinking holds promise in the classroom across various levels of implementation" (Pousley, 2017; see also Luka, 2014; Rauth, Koppen, Jobst, & Meinel, 2010).

There are many strategies and activities that support design thinking. For example, at the University of Arkansas, STEM challenges were created that work as design activities with groups of students. Initially, the students read *The Three Billy Goat's Gruff*, which is a Norwegian fairy tale about three characters who attempt to cross a bridge. A hungry and mean troll lives under the bridge, and he would love to catch and eat any goat that attempts to cross the bridge. After reading the story, the following challenge was given:

> You decide to help the billy goats reach the opposite side of the creek so they can eat. You must create a model structure to help the billy goats get from one side to the other while using the design loop and only the materials provided. [The teacher provides] model billy goats, with specific weights, that your bridge must be able to withstand (Juliani, 2019).

Another design thinking activity is "Book in an Hour" Activity (via All Who Wonder)." This is a group-design challenge, but also is useful as an individual challenge:

> Give a group a book (fiction or non-fiction). Then you break them up into smaller groups (or individuals) to read different parts of the book. Each group (or person) has to read and then create an overview/trailer of their part of the book to share chronologically with the rest of the class. Here the design really starts with the creative process driving how you share the information, plot, characters, etc.

These and other fun activities can be adapted to elementary and secondary school settings and to professional development workshops.

The essence of design thinking connects nicely with the many critical thinking strategies and activities presented in this book. When educators embrace and respect students' desire to engage in any aspect of the creative process, students are more likely to be receptive and to channel their energy into a collaborative problem-solving structure like design thinking or comparable processes. Moving in this direction requires open-minded educators who not only support HITS but also provide reminders that the development of these skills serves the best interests of humanity when students' creative energy is guided by moral commitment (Noddings & Brooks, 2017).

Humor and Creative Problem Solving

Another dimension of creativity is humor, and research supports positive connections between creative problem solving and humor (Korovkin & Nikiforova, 2014, 2015; Martin, 2006). Insight problem solving and jokes are also enjoyable, especially when those involved with a problem find a solution to it and when those engaged with a joke understand the joke and are surprised by it. Canestrari et al. (2018) present this perspective in the context of a "general" theory of the pleasures of the mind (Kubovy, 1999).

According to Spencer (2019), "When teachers smile, laugh, and goof off, they are modeling creativity." Spencer believes that humor is vitally important for a creative classroom, and he suggests five ways that humor can boost creative thinking and problem solving:

1. It encourages creative risk-taking because it gives "students permission to be goofy and nerdy and whimsical. And, in the process, it [gives] people permission to have their own unique creative voice."
2. It develops divergent thinking because "most humor is a chance to see things from a new perspective. Prop

humor is essentially a divergent thinking exercise in using an item the wrong way. A pun is essentially a chance to use language incorrectly in order to get a laugh."
3. It models curiosity and playfulness. Teachers who use humor, especially observational humor, are modeling a specific type of curiosity and also a readiness "to look at life from a different angle. While this might not seem like an inherently creative act, curiosity is often the starting point for creativity. At some point, you move from questioning and exploring into making."
4. It boosts creative problem solving, and it seems to support "the connection between improvisational humor and things like empathy, problem solving, and divergent thinking."
5. It leads to creative fluency by affording opportunities "to be creative in the small things ... if we embrace the goofy and silly and ridiculous and humorous ... we have embraced that mindset that allows us to be creative in the big things ... this actually leads to creative fluency."

Because children and adolescents watch lots of sitcom humor on TV, YouTube videos, and other outlets, they sometimes experience lots of negative put-down humor. Although some of these sources are not good role models, they still serve a purpose for promoting critical thinking. For example, using a graphic organizer for comparing and contrasting, the teacher can engage students in a thoughtful discussion of positive versus negative humor, with examples of each, and can guide students to develop a working definition of these two types of humor. Then, the teacher models a basic variation of content analysis research methodology by showing students how to summarize a form of content by counting or tallying aspects of the content. Next, the teacher selects a sitcom program and shows students how to apply this methodology to the program as she or he tallies examples of the characters' positive and negative verbal and nonverbal behavior. The characters in the sitcom will predictably make humorous (sometimes sarcastic) comments and engage in similar nonverbal actions; meanwhile, the teacher will tally them in the graphic organizer while metacognitively thinking aloud. Afterward, everyone discusses the results, which involve not only the numerical tallies but also qualitative aspects of the types of verbal and nonverbal humor that was used. As an enrichment follow-up activity, individual students or small groups select a program in which they are interested, tally the examples of positive and negative behavior, and indicate the kinds of humor that were observed. Discussing the results can increase transfer of learning to new contexts, and an important aspect of transfer value should reflect humane considerations for helping students to realize that put-down humor should not be used intentionally to hurt anyone. This stance is in line with maintaining a moral commitment to teaching and learning that serves the best interests of humanity, and students in elementary, middle, and high schools are in need of this important reminder.

Universities, Corporate Models, and Whistleblowing

Another important consideration for enhancing transfer of learning is to immerse secondary-level and college students in the issue of universities adopting a business model, which might result in the need for whistleblowing. The issue might read as follows:

> "I want to know have you ever seen the rain?" With no drama intended, John Fogerty's lyrics metaphorically reflect lots of rain and pain for academics and students nationwide, as they see their universities morphed into a corporate model that highlights the near death of intellectual and personal growth. The model emphasizes

financial priorities to the extent that these priorities often negate effective teaching and learning. Faculty, students, and parents need to be aware of the current realities of the corporate model and their negative impact on the academy.

Moving in this direction requires substantive and eloquent whistleblowing, which has been an admired event in American history. From whistleblower laws passed in 1778 by the Continental Congress to Abraham Lincoln's support of such laws in 1863, Americans have generally celebrated the value of whistleblowing. In his thoughtful essay "Sounding the Alarm" (2019b) and his authoritative book *Crisis of Conscience: Whistleblowing in an Age of Fraud* (2019a), Tom Mueller elaborates the immensity of fraudulent practices perpetrated by corporations, government officials, and others, and he stresses the need for courageous individuals to expose the wrongdoing that they encounter.

After reading and discussing the whistleblower laws of 1778 and Tom Mueller's current perspectives, students can engage in extensive research and write critical papers that probably have relevance to their lives as college students or future postsecondary students. Specifically, students might analyze, synthesize, and verify related issues and incorporate them into their writing. The following questions might provide guidance:

- If eliminating tenure is an important part of the higher education corporate model, what percentage of college and university instructors in the United States are not tenure-track faculty? What types of positions have replaced tenure-track faculty? What are the pros and cons of these replacement positions?
- If the university corporate model involves cutting support staff—advisers, secretaries, administrative

assistants—are they essential for responding to the needs of students, faculty, chairpersons, and deans? If so, then why and how are they necessary?
- If expecting a shrinking faculty and support staff to provide extra help for comprehensive accreditation activities, grant proposals, and other time-consuming responsibilities, how will this impact teaching and learning?
- If university instructional programs are eliminated—majors, minors—how will this affect students' career aspirations and choices?
- If increased class size is the result of other course sections that were eliminated, how does this affect the quality and quantity of essential standards, activities and assignments?
- If the university corporate model promulgates a philosophy of giving the customer what he or she wants, what impact will this have on the core curriculum, liberal arts requirements, and higher grades that are undeserved?
- If aspects of the corporate-based agenda dominate the economics and power structure of higher education, to what extent will this business mindset affect academic freedom, academic integrity, and academic standards?
- If students have special needs, what percentage of their tuition is used to accommodate these needs via special services, highly competent and caring counselors, extended/instructive office hours for individuals who need extra help, writing/learning centers that are congruent with professors' requirements, and other sources of support? What is the graduation rate for first-generation students? Because first-generation students have a marginalized voice in higher education, what opportunities are provided so they can express their voice?

♦ If whistleblowing is used as a response to the university corporate model, how effective will it be? What communication sources will be most credible: infomercials? articles? editorials? Op-Ed pieces? YouTube videos? Vimeo productions? Other outlets? In your judgment, what increases their credibility?

As students engage in related discussions and activities, they should have options to choose areas they wish to research, analyze, and write about. They also need the freedom to work individually, or they might decide to work in pairs or in small groups that complement and support collaborative efforts. Choice is important in both content and process.

Propaganda Devices

Television programs, Internet websites, magazines, newspapers, and other sources are often blitzed with commercial advertisements. The sponsors' intent is obvious: to persuade consumers to buy their products or to agree with their ideologies. Students benefit from opportunities to interpret the motivations and techniques of the sponsors, and learning about propaganda devices can be helpful. There are many categories of propaganda, and some are easily applied to students' interest in popular culture. They include (but are not limited to) glittering generalities, name calling, loaded terms, card stacking, bandwagon, plain folks, testimonial, and transfer. Students enjoy researching definitions of these and other propaganda techniques and applying them to commercial advertisements and political ads. Although propaganda definitions abound, Smith (2021) posits that propaganda is a systematic attempt to manipulate other people's attitudes, actions, and beliefs by means of symbols, such as words, gestures, music, hairstyles, clothing, designs, banners, monuments, and insignia on postage stamps and coins. According to Smith, what distinguishes propaganda from casual conversation is a disposition of deliberateness and a relatively strong emphasis on manipulation.

    Propagandists have a specified goal or set of goals. To achieve these, they deliberately select facts, arguments, and displays of symbols and present them in ways they think will have the most effect. To maximize effect, they may omit or distort pertinent facts or simply lie, and they may try to divert the attention of the reactors (the people they are trying to sway) from everything but their own propaganda.

Complementing Smith's perspective on propaganda are peer-reviewed publications and Internet websites that provide support for students' research, and a sampling includes "Teaching about Propaganda: An Examination of the Historical Roots of Media Literacy" (Hobbs & McGee, 2014), "Promiscuity Propaganda: Access to Information and Services Does Not Lead to Increases in Sexual Activity" (Dreweke, 2019), *Critical Thinking: Recognizing Propaganda Techniques and Errors of Faulty Logic* (Cuesta College, 2021), *Propaganda Techniques to Recognize* (UVM, n.d.), and *Propaganda: The Art of Persuasion* (MCA, n.d.). When students become immersed in these and other explorations, they come to realize that more than one propaganda device might be used because commercial sponsors and speech writers often do not adhere to one device; they often use several techniques because their main motivation is to persuade the audience.

    As learners discuss and share examples of propaganda, they benefit from guidance in analyzing and synthesizing related process and content, in rating the effectiveness of the commercials, and in supporting their position as to why the propaganda is or is not successful. Specifically, learners profit from opportunities to engage in critical thinking of their selected commercial by responding to—and providing evidence for—thoughtful questions like the following adapted here:

- what do you notice about the language and images that are used?
- what are your eyes drawn to?
- how would you describe the music used?
- what are the primary colors?
- where is the placement of the logo or the slogan?
- how does the ad try to assure that you'll remember it? (Just Add Students, 2020).

These are interesting (and serious) activities and responses that not only enhance the application of HITS but also support a deeper understanding of how multimodal texts are used.

This comprehensive section focused on the channel-surfing activity (Noddings & Brooks, 2017); the ThinkCERCA platform (Cramer & Hubers, 2016); the productive group work for the 1935 Social Security Act (Vaca, Lapp, & Fisher, 2011); the Sports and Society elective class (West, 2019); the pairing of easy and challenging literature (Palumbo & Sanacore, 2013); the pairing of traditional books, graphic books, and film versions; the connections between children's literature and inferential discussions (Kelly & Moses, 2018); the painting writing, writing painting context (Martens et al., 2018); the links between reflective practice and service learning (CCESI, 2020); the immigrants, jobs, and crime collaborative projects; the important relationships among independent reading, vocabulary development, and comprehension; the creativity considerations for problem solving; the value of humor for creativity and problem solving (Spencer, 2019); the issue of universities, corporate models, and whistleblowing; and propaganda devices (Just Add Students, 2020).

These are thoughtful and effective approaches for transferring critical thinking to important content. As educators support these and other extended approaches, they realize that the critical thinking process does not occur automatically. If it were that easy, most people would probably be critical thinkers. Realistically, developing open-mindedness and demonstrating a commitment to critical thinking require time and experience with both direct instruction and student-centered learning, as students become immersed in content-based assignments and related civil dialogue.

5
Other Strategies and Activities That Support Transfer of Learning

Before, during, and after extended approaches, including those presented in the previous chapter, students also benefit from engaging in a variety of strategies and activities that further support application and transfer of learning. Teachers therefore need to expand their repertoire of instructional practices that not only complement well-planned instructional lessons and thematic units but also support teachable moments. Consider the following enhancements:

Inquiry Dialogue

This type of talk supports students' efforts to work collaboratively as they pursue the "truth" by searching for the most reasonable answer to a question (Walton, 1998). "As students discuss big questions during inquiry dialogue, they take part in a genuine quest for truth and develop personally meaningful judgments" (Reznitskaya & Wilkinson, 2017/2018, p. 35). During these intellectually rigorous discussions, inquiry dialogue is more likely to fulfill its truth-seeking mission when teachers engage the participants in weighing the strengths and flaws of one another's arguments based on the following criteria:

1. Diversity of perspectives: We explore different perspectives together.
2. Clarity: We are clear in the language and structure of our arguments.
3. Acceptability of reasons and evidence: We use reasons and evidence that are well-examined and accurate.
4. Logical validity: We are logical in the way we connect our positions, reasons, and evidence (Reznitskaya & Wilkinson, 2017, p. 36; see also Reznitskaya & Wilkinson, 2017/2018).

In carrying out the collaborative essence of inquiry dialogue, an important point to remember is that the teacher supports students in applying these four criteria as she or he emphasizes shared ownership. This helps students to feel a sense of belonging, to have productive group sessions, and to agree and disagree with civility.

More Open-Ended Questions

Another complement to our mission of promoting higher-level thinking, especially for high school and college students, is increasing critical-thinking questions that are open-ended, challenging, and require genuine inquiry, analysis, or assessment. For example:

- What is your interpretation/analysis of this passage/data/argument?
- What are your reasons for favoring that interpretation/analysis? What is your evidence?
- How well does your interpretation/analysis handle the complexities of the passage/data/argument?
- What is another interpretation/analysis of the passage/data/argument? Any others?
- What are the implications of each interpretation/analysis?
- Let's look at all the interpretations/analyses and evaluate them. How strong is the evidence for each one?
- How honestly and impartially are you representing the other interpretations/analyses? Do you have a vested interest in one interpretation/analysis over another?
- What additional information would help us to narrow down our interpretations/analyses? (Nilson, 2018)

Increasing Wait Time

These and similar questions are more apt to motivate students' engagement and deep thinking when the teacher provides more time to process thoughts. One consideration is for teachers to "pause with purpose after every question, and again after every answer. That second pause helps other students reconsider the question and reflect on the first answer" (Abla, 2019).

Because everyone processes information in unique ways, students benefit from getting into the habit of waiting, reflecting, and responding in ways that encourage thoughtful discussions rather than impulsive responses. A general guideline to consider is: the deeper the question, the longer the wait time. The importance of wait time can be clarified when it is framed in an exclusive versus inclusive context. For example:

> **Exclusive time**: The teacher asks questions, quickly redirects the questions to other students, or rephrases the questions. (This quick pacing of questions prevents some students from reflecting and then responding. Only students with a rapid or impulsive way of thinking are able to participate in related discussions.)
>
> **Inclusive time**: The teacher poses questions, encourages students to formulate their own questions, and provides sufficient wait time—between three and fifteen seconds. (Increasing wait time provides opportunities for all children to engage in reflection, elaboration, and higher-level thinking. This positive context builds self-esteem as it stimulates a variety of responses from a diversity of learners and encourages students to develop the habit of asking their own questions.) (Sanacore, 2005, p. 103).

More Thoughtful, Inclusive Questions

In addition to wait time, students are always observing us, including **how** we ask questions, and they probably will apply similar types of questions when reading and writing independently. Thoughtful and challenging questions nurture students' HITS, increase their self-efficacy, build their sense of self-determination, and motivate their participation during class discussions (Sanacore, 2008). Furthermore, challenging questions can help reluctant learners to attain high expectations. Although unmotivated learners are as individual in their unwillingness to learn as they are in their motivation to learn, some commonalities exist. According to Protheroe (2004), reluctant learners avoid challenges, are satisfied with just getting by, and do not complete tasks. Yet, they are capable of excelling but do not seem concerned about achieving in school. "The essential point to remember is that a student's motivation can vary, depending on the subject, setting, and teaching style" (Shore, 2001, p. 20).

The problem of unmotivated learners is evident in all grades, but it is most apparent in the middle grades when these students are blitzed with physical, emotional, and social changes and challenges. Simultaneously, middle school academic demands increase, which can exacerbate students' frustration as they attempt to fulfill academic requirements and personal priorities. "Fitting in" with peers is vitally important for tweens, so it should be no surprise that a combination of factors is causing academic enthusiasm to fade. If lack of interest becomes deep-rooted and continues into high school, some of these students might never accept the value of critical thinking and might even drop out of school. Expecting students to grow from reluctance to inspiration requires teachers who move beyond extrinsically oriented token rewards to intrinsically centered teaching and learning that afford opportunities to respond to deep thinking in personal ways (Sanacore, 2008). Supporting this outcome is not easy for both students and teachers, but it can become reality when the learning environment is both encouraging and challenging.

As teachers move in this direction, they need to plan challenging lessons that foster personal connections to learning, including thoughtful questions that motivate a variety of responses from a diversity of learners. To begin, teachers should determine if the questions are exclusive or inclusive. Exclusive questions elicit precise responses from a select group of learners, while inclusive questions provide opportunities for rich discussion among all students. What follows are examples of exclusive and inclusive questions that are adapted from Sanacore (2005) and Palumbo and Sanacore (2013) and are applied to Patricia Polacco's *Pink and Say*. This poignant, historical picture book, which is acceptable and respectable for older students, is based on the true story of Pinkus Aylee, his mom Moe Moe Bay, and Sheldon Russell Curtis, and what they encountered during the American Civil War. Intermediate and middle-level learners can engage in serious conversations about this powerful book, especially when they are guided with thoughtful, inclusive questions. For clarification and application, let's view the exclusive versus inclusive perspectives:

Exclusive questions for responding to text: In the story *Pink and Say*, who are the main characters? What problems did they face? When did these problems occur? Where did these problems occur? (These basic questions tend to support a literal level of understanding. Because they promote a boring discussion, fewer students are apt to participate.)

Inclusive questions for responding to text: In the story *Pink and Say*, think beyond the ideas and events that are presented. If you were Pink or Say or Moe Moe Bay, how would you have approached the problems they faced? What would you have learned about yourself from your approach to the problems? What difficulties would you have encountered as you attempted to solve the problems? What would you have learned about yourself from the ways in which you handled these difficulties? Would you have dealt with the problems successfully? Why? (These questions foster personal responses. Because no right or wrong answers are required, students are motivated to share and verify their responses.)

Learning Journals

Another source of support that helps to extend critical thinking to other venues is a learning journal, which is simply a continuous collection of writing for learning. In this context, learning journals reflect personal and academic thoughts written in different types of text, including traditional print, digital text, blogs, artistic illustrations, and other multimodal forms. Their purpose is to stimulate, deepen, or extend learning. Heick (2019) suggests 20 types of learning journals, a few of which are adapted here for promoting critical thinking and transferring it to different content areas.

Question Journal: This type of journal highlights the importance of inquiry by providing students with opportunities to ask and refine their questions. This type of reflection can also result in metacognitive thinking as students write about their increased awareness and understanding of their thought processes and of the need to change or adapt their thinking related to problem solving.

I Wonder ... Journal: Students benefit from experiences that provide time and space for imaginative entries that are based on wondering and musing. Examples might include "I wonder ... if literary symbolism is what makes hip-hop so powerful or if it's more word play and sounds?" or "I wonder ... if Pythagoras based his theory on something he had recently learned himself?"

Visualization Journal: This type of journal promotes specific and acute imaginings or conceptions of knowledge. Students could create visual analogies or metaphors of a learned concept via drawings, paintings, cartoons, caricatures, photographs, and other multimodal texts.

Concept/Example Journal: Students benefit from activities that foster thinking through abstract concepts and related examples. In the science of physics, students could write about the concept of gravity and its connections to angular momentum or centrifugal force. This writing could take the form of print, diagrams, and other graphic representations.

These and other journal formats are useful for helping students to reflect on the quality of their learning. To further support the effectiveness of learning journals, Heick (2019) provides a caution: "A common tendency for journal entries is to become a mere log of events rather than a reflective activity in which students consider the service experience in the context of learning objectives. Guidance is needed to help students link personal learning with course content."

A meaningful way of dissuading mere-log-of-events journal entries is to encourage deeper, critical reflections in learning journals. At the very least, this involves interactive responses that move beyond any type of text—for example, traditional, multimodal—and recognize that all types of texts and all consumers of texts are not neutral. One approach to deconstruct texts and, simultaneously, to explore counter-narratives is to pose critical-lens questions, such as the following:

- How does this text center certain ideas, values, or groups while marginalizing others?
- What does the author want me to think, feel, or believe?
- How might this text help me identify or challenge my perceptions and assumptions?
- How is this text attempting to influence my thinking about this topic?
- How does this text perpetuate stereotypes?
- Who does this text privilege? How is that privilege leveraged?
- Who is silenced or underrepresented in this text? What purpose is served by that omission?

♦ What is the counter-narrative? (Kelly, Laminack, & Gould, 2020, p. 298).

Although these critical-thinking questions help to reveal a keen awareness of biases and assumptions in both texts and readers, they represent only one piece of the broader critical-literacy framework. An inclusive perspective to consider is that critical literacy is most effective when it is connected to teaching and learning as a way of viewing the world with a lens that illuminates and clarifies what is heard, viewed, read, or written. "It is an awareness, a consciousness about perspective, power, and intention. To become critically literate is to develop the ability to see and think about the story not told, the voice not honored, the information withheld, the message muted" (Kelly, Laminack, & Gould, 2020, p. 298; see also Laminack & Kelly, 2019). When connected to learning journals, critical literacy and critical thinking provide opportunities to engage in deeper, refined, personal thought during the writing process.

Extended assignments help students apply critical and creative insights that result in transfer of learning, especially when these insights are connected to collaborative inquiry dialogue, more inclusive wait time, more inclusive questions, learning journals, and other thoughtful activities that support the value of HITS. When students have opportunities to transfer deep thinking to a variety of new and meaningful contexts, they are able to observe with a critical eye the positions and intent of politicians, political analysts, writers, speakers, neighbors, friends, parents, and almost anyone with conservative, moderate, liberal, independent, and other perspectives. This critical awareness increases the chances of young citizens becoming strong, independent thinkers who are less likely to be swayed by questionable motives, agendas, and rhetoric.

6
The Value of Hard Work

Achieving critical awareness and becoming independent thinkers require hard work. In a related study, data from 1347 high school graduates were released by Achieve (2014), a nonprofit, nonpartisan, and independent education reform organization. Those who responded to the survey included Hispanic Americans, African Americans, whites, females, and males. Disaggregated by ethnicity, 50% of Hispanic Americans and 53% of African Americans responded affirmatively to the question: "If my high school had demanded more, set higher academic standards, and raised expectations of the course work and studying necessary to earn a diploma, I am certain I would have worked harder." Another study (Murillo & Schall, 2016) provided further support for understanding and meeting the learning needs of ethnic-minority students. This qualitative study focused on Mexican-origin, first-generation college freshmen and their high school experiences. Among the findings is that the freshmen did not view themselves as well prepared for college. Students highlighted high school classroom practices (e.g., test preparation activities and worksheets) that were unrelated to their interests; they also indicated that their high school teachers did not challenge them to learn. Furthermore, they reported a contrast in high school and college reading expectations, in that their high school reading was narrowly focused and boring, whereas their college texts required higher-level thinking skills. Also problematic for these freshmen were their college instructors who did not provide adequate support for navigating college-level texts. These and other studies suggest high school students are more apt to work hard and be better prepared for college rigor when their learning environment is stimulating, challenging, engaging, and supportive (Hidden Curriculum, 2014). Moving in this direction is essential for narrowing achievement gaps that prevent all learners, especially low-income students, from attaining success.

Students' hard work, however, should be complemented by high school counselors and administrators who research thoroughly the colleges to which students apply to determine if they provide effective support systems that result in academic success and graduation rates comparable to the state graduation rate. At the very least, high school seniors have a right to know the demographic backgrounds of students currently attending their preferred college and the college's graduation rates disaggregated by ethnicity. Seniors also deserve substantiated information about their preferred college's mentoring and related support systems (if any) that work congruently to support success; these include professors and mentors reinforcing deep writing, reading, and note-taking of difficult texts, resulting in productive challenges instead of destructive frustrations (Sanacore & Palumbo, 2015; Snow, 2013). If this type of support can be substantiated, it would help to negate one of the findings in the Murillo and Schall (2016) study, in which college freshmen reported that their professors did not provide enough support for navigating college-level texts.

Overall, supporting students' work ethic through the grades nurtures education for life because it sets a positive foundation for continued growth and development into adulthood. When students' hard work is rewarded with success, they realize a sense of accomplishment which, in turn, helps them to continue valuing hard work. This big-picture perspective is vitally important for their emotional and academic future, but moving in this direction requires the support of teachers who are genuinely committed to caring for their students. Seven decades ago, Highet (1950) provided valuable insights for understanding the values and emotions of teaching. In his timeless book *The Art of Teaching*, he posited that effective teaching requires deeply knowing and liking students and continuing to learn about them, as they demonstrate unique (and sometimes peculiar) thoughts and emotions. Highet's perspective was clear: "If you do not actually like boys and girls, or young men and young women, give up teaching" (p. 24).

On certain days, however, such intense caring can be emotionally and physically exhausting for teachers, reflecting the good, the bad, and the ugly (Winograd, 2003). But deep caring can also be rewarding, especially if we remember Mother Teresa's deep level of caring and loving when she said: "I have found the paradox that if I love until it hurts, then there is no hurt, but only more love" (cited in Sanacore, 2012, p. 194). While seemingly idealistic in school settings, caring teachers and administrators can experience a variation of this stance when they observe at the end of the school year that students they deliberately and consistently supported throughout the year have demonstrated substantial growth and development, both emotionally and academically. Highet's and Mother Teresa's perspectives challenge teachers to question their daily roles as either a teacher of content or a teacher of students. Aiming for a consistent balance of these roles is best for students' growth and development. Additional insights about supporting success for all students, especially ethnic minority learners, can be found in professional literature related to mentoring, *My Brother's Keeper*, and similar initiatives (Hammond & Senor, 2014; Obama, 2014; Sanacore, 2017).

7
Reflections on Critical Thinking

Indeed, helping all students to become critical, independent thinkers is not easy and requires hard work, patience, and perseverance from both teachers and students because this type of change represents a major cultural shift in values and attitudes. Achieving independence as a critical thinker is also difficult because:

> it goes against our natural tendency to want to perceive selectively and confirm what we already 'know' to be true. Therefore, critical thinking involves character as well as cognition. Students must be inclined to pursue 'truth' over their own biases, persist through challenges, assess their own thinking fairly, and abandon mistaken reasoning for new and more valid ways of thinking. These intellectual 'virtues' don't come easily or naturally (Nilson, 2018; see also Abrami et al., 2008; Kahneman, 2011; Kenrick, Cohen, Neuberg, & Cialdini, 2018; Kruger & Dunning, 1999).

Challenges of Political Partisanship

Exacerbating this perspective are issues of political partisanship, in which those with limited ability or expertise believe they have substantial ability or expertise. This overestimation, or cognitive bias, "occurs as a result of the fact that they don't have enough knowledge to know they don't have enough knowledge" (Azarian, 2018). When this aspect of the "Dunning-Kruger effect" is applied to the realm of political knowledge, a better understanding of partisanship emerges; that is, when a greater emphasis is placed on political affiliation, people who demonstrate little political knowledge tend to exaggerate their expertise even more (Anson, 2018). Dunning puts it this way:

> In studies in my research lab, people with severe gaps in knowledge and expertise typically fail to recognize how

little they know and how badly they perform. To sum it up, the knowledge and intelligence that are required to be good at a task are often the same qualities needed to recognize that one is *not* good at that task—and if one lacks such knowledge and intelligence, one remains ignorant that one is not good at that task. This includes political judgment (Dunning, 2016).

Understanding These Challenges

As we reflect on people's partisan politics accompanied by their limited political knowledge, we come to realize the educational challenges of helping students achieve mastery of critical thinking. Samet (2015) suggests viewing such mastery as an artful synthesis of theoretical knowledge and practical experience in the development of superb judgment. In his thoughtful essay "Of Books," sixteenth-century French philosopher Michel Eyquem de Montaigne was strongly committed to this balance: "Knowledge and truth can lodge within us without judgement; judgement can do so without them: indeed, recognizing our ignorance is one of the surest and most beautiful witnesses to our judgement that I can find" (cited in Samet, 2015, pp. 186–187). In another essay, "On Educating Children," Montaigne stated that when our students engage in conversation, they need guidance in understanding that admitting an error in their arguments is an act of integrity and justice and that these are the primary qualities students should pursue. "Stubbornness and rancour are vulgar qualities, visible in common souls whereas to think again, to change one's mind and to give up a bad case in the heat of the argument are rare qualities showing strength and wisdom" (cited in Samet, 2015, p. 384).

Montaigne elaborated these views by stating that we should consider everything provisionally and questioningly in our emotional, social, and intellectual lives (Bakewell, 2010; Countryman, 2012). Taken to an extreme, however, this view might be misinterpreted as an inkling of the nihilistic philosophy, which indicates life has no purpose or meaning because nothing really exists or can be known (Bonagura, 2019). According to John Paul II, nihilists believe "life is no more than an occasion of sensations and experiences in which the ephemeral has pride of place. Nihilism is at the root of the widespread mentality which claims that a definitive commitment should no longer be made because everything is fleeting and provisional" (cited in Bonagura, 2019, p. 34).

Importance of Cooperation

Considering the complicated realities of being human and the complexities of thinking critically, students who work collaboratively come to realize that we need one another and that we are meant to be a community (Servant, 2019). With this sense of belonging, students are more apt to embrace the intricate process of making judgments when their participation in critical thinking activities is not competitive but instead is guided by moral imperatives. If students insist on being competitive—for example, in formal debates about political rhetoric—the teacher can help them to realize the difference between competitive competition and cooperative competition, with the former focused on winning and the latter focused on producing better citizens who are dedicated to supporting a better democratic society for all citizens. In his thought-provoking essay "The 'Go-Getter' Spirit: Competition Thrives on Insecurity, Works Against Democracy," anthropologist Ashley Montagu (1952) maintained a strong belief:

> that such greatness as America has achieved it has achieved not through competition but in spite of competition; that the life-blood of a nation is not commerce through competition, but social welfare through cooperation; that, indeed, commerce through competition can be the death of a nation, and that only through the

dominance of the cooperative motive can any people or nation survive.

Complementing the intent of cooperative competition is the value of cooperative argumentation, which highlights consensus instead of winning. This model of deliberative community suggests that everyone's knowledge, partly the result of life experiences, is treated with respect as peers listen attentively to others' viewpoints. In his essay "How Does Your Positionality Bias Your Epistemology?" Takacs (2003) posits that when students' listening is genuine, they "listen to understand, not to judge or triumph ... Rather than convincing others of the inevitability of your position, when you listen to others' perspectives, you may question your assumptions and lower the barriers to be able to reach consensus" (p. 32). This asset model (of multiculturalism) provides students with opportunities to connect their life experiences to their viewpoints as an integral part of reaching consensus. Students also engage in deeper discussions and analyses that challenge norms and assumptions, and they "gnaw on how positionality biases epistemology" (p. 35). Furthermore, they benefit from opportunities to connect their social and political context to their justified beliefs versus opinions as they become immersed in personal explorations of classism, racism, sexism, homophobia, and other vitally important issues and differences that can reflect disadvantages, hardships, and vulnerabilities. When we consistently engage in understanding how our positionality biases our epistemology, we refine aspects of critical thinking, while "we greet the world with respect, interact with others to explore and cherish their differences, and live life with a fuller sense of self as part of a web of community" (p. 38).

Not surprisingly, this humanistic direction reinforces the value of culturally responsive sustaining education (CRSE), as this framework supports educators' efforts to create student-centered learning environments that "affirm racial, linguistic, and cultural identities; prepare students for rigor and independent learning; develop students' abilities to connect across lines of difference; elevate historically marginalized voices; and empower students as agents of social change" (NYSED, n.d.). Not surprisingly, CRSE is supported not only by state education departments nationwide but also by professional organizations. The International Literacy Association, for example, provides ILA Digital Events, and a recent one focused on the theme "Culturally Relevant and Responsive: Literacy Instruction in 2021 and Beyond." This three-hour event was designed to guide literacy educators and leaders to create inclusive school settings that respect and reflect all learners. The panel consisted of Gloria Ladson-Billings, Pamela Mason, Lucia Cardenas Curiel, Matthey Kay, and Guofang Li. This panel addressed the following areas:

- How educators can identify the effects their own backgrounds and implicit biases have on teaching and learning
- How to question pedagogy and policies that negatively impact learner outcomes
- Proactive steps literacy and school leaders can take to dismantle oppressive systems.

Culturally responsive sustaining education is a useful framework for decreasing, and eventually eradicating, ethnic minority prejudice. A vitally important (but sometimes missing) part of understanding bigotry is the hurt that results from it. In *Tears We Cannot Stop: A Sermon to White America*, Dyson (2017) provides many poignant examples of the devastating effects of bigotry and racism. One such example is when his 8-year-old daughter, Maisha, traveled with family friends to Disney World in Florida. While relaxing in the hotel swimming pool with two friends, a little girl swam by them and said in a matter-of-fact tone, "Niggers." The three African American girls responded by stiffening their backs, tightening their facial gestures, and spontaneously bursting out in laughter. According to Dyson (2017, p. 25):

> It was an all-too-familiar gesture of self-defense. It was a way to stave off the creep of hate inside your brain. This is what race hate does to our kids. It often attacks them without warning. It makes them develop a tough exterior to combat the flow of racial insanity into their minds ... Maisha and her friends were wise enough ... to know that the little white girl was repeating what she heard, that she was reflecting what she'd been taught. Lessons of race that are learned early are hard to get rid of later on. Often they harden into warped perceptions of black folk. Those perceptions turn to cudgels that are wielded against us when we least expect it.

This poignant response reflects not only the hurt that results from racial and ethnic prejudice but also the need for culturally responsive sustaining education and its important role in building cooperative communities that work toward eradicating all kinds of prejudice.

Another vulnerable group of citizens who encounter bigotry is the LGBTQ community, and a recent Gallup update on lesbian, gay, bisexual, and transgender identification indicates that 5.6% of adults in the United States (ages 18 and older) consider themselves LGBT. This estimate reflects an increase from 4.5%, based on Gallup's previous 2017 data (Jones, 2021). The prejudicial issues they confront include (but are not limited to) declarations that transgender people should not be permitted to serve in the U.S. military; determinations that Title VII of the Civil Rights Act does not prohibit discrimination of transgender people in the workplace; definitions of gender as a biological, immutable condition determined by genitalia at birth; and proclamations that LGBTQ people are sinners. As adolescent and adult members of the LGBTQ community realize these intentional actions against them, they must wonder about how people with power and fellow citizens have not only violated their rights but also abandoned them. This is a frightening position to be in as these younger and older Americans seem to be continuously pitted against their straight peers, instead of feeling free to be themselves in a so-called free democratic society. Such antiquated, regressive thinking will inevitably result in abuses both in the workplace and in school. From a learning perspective, students' anxiety about their LGBTQ identity is likely to reduce their cognitive capacity because their intellectual processing will be blurred with intense feelings of nonacceptance, of being bullied, and of engaging in fight-or-flight behavior. This type of gender confusion torments many adolescents today:

> They are surrounded by comments and stories in the news and social media about the lives and experiences of lesbians, gays, bisexuals, and queer and transgender people, and teachers and [parents] are not always well prepared to address the questions they have. Indeed, they may need help in formulating their questions and finding ways in which to ask them. We want to encourage free conversation, but we also want to protect students against making disclosures they may later regret (Noddings & Brooks, 2017, p. 156).

For additional insights about gender worldwide, read the special issue of *National Geographic* (2017), which highlights social, cultural, political, and biological aspects of gender.

As educators strive to create cooperative communities, they increase the chances of young citizens making better and more caring judgments about valuing one another. This asset model supports a "web of community" and establishes a positive foundation for emotional and social growth, thereby building confidence for risk-taking and for engaging in HITS. The model, however, needs to be reinforced in developmentally appropriate ways as children and adolescents become immersed in content area discussions, activities, and projects. An important part of these efforts is to remind young citizens that empathy is needed, that we are motivated by feelings, and that feeling for another's hurt, fear, or need drives us to action. Children can more easily move toward this humanistic direction when their school and home environment is packed with genuine love and caring (Sanacore, 2004, 2012). "This suggests strongly that the task of teachers and parents is to educate the hearts and feelings of our children, not simply their minds ... Children must be reminded to notice, understand, and respond appropriately to the feelings of others ... in this context, we are referring to what is felt, or should be felt, by the moral agent" (Noddings & Brooks, 2017, pp. 14–15; see also Hoffman, 2000; Hume, 1983/1751; Noddings, 2013/1984). When children believe that adults in their lives love and care for them, they are more likely to take risks as they attempt to better understand and respond to the perspectives of others, including their emotional, social, and academic well-being.

Supporting this stance is the wisdom of Rev. Dr. Martin Luther King, Jr., who strongly supported the power of empathy and its connection to love and caring. Reverend King believed that what is needed in (political) leadership "is a realization that power without love is reckless and abusive and that love without power is sentimental and anemic. Power at its best is love implementing the demands of justice, and justice at its best is love correcting everything that stands against love" (King, 1967). Interestingly, in the movie *Star Trek IV: The Voyage Home* (Bennett & Nimoy, 1986), Spock attempts to communicate with a computer that asks him, "How do you feel?" Spock, of course, is baffled because he considers the question to be illogical. As the movie plot develops, Spock, at least, attempts to understand and respond favorably to a sense of empathy, while some political leaders continue to use rhetoric and actions to negate both logic and empathy. The questionable intent of some leaders, journalists, neighbors, and others necessitates a call to action to make critical thinking a strong part of all school curricula. Motivating students to engage in critical thinking across the curriculum is more apt to be effective when the learning and teaching context supports personalized learning.

Encouraging Intrinsic Motivation

Although instructional strategies for promoting personal and individual responses to learning have already been suggested, students need more opportunities to become immersed in activities that highlight learning engagement and intrinsic motivation. While not negating the value of extrinsic motivation, students also benefit from experiences that stimulate an inner desire and excitement about learning. The previous suggestions for promoting and applying critical thinking reflect a balance of both extrinsic and intrinsic perspectives, as they encourage teacher-directed instruction (which is based mostly in behaviorist and extrinsically motivated approaches) and student-centered learning (which is based mostly in constructivist and intrinsically motivated activities).

Regrettably, in the 2016 Gallup Student Poll, the researchers found that students' engagement seems to wane significantly as they progress through the grades. For example, of the surveyed students in grades 5–12 in about 3000 schools, 74% of fifth graders and only 34% of twelfth graders were engaged with school (Calderon & Yu, 2017). These findings should be constant reminders for teachers and administrators that their N–12 students need a better balance of instructional practices if they are expected to eventually graduate from high school and demonstrate not only serious interest in lifelong learning but also ability to engage independently in critical thinking. This balance is essential for effective learning and teaching, especially in the practical context of school curricula and state standards. Yet, the balance rarely occurs because most schools use direct instruction disproportionately when compared with personalized learning and other considerations for enhancing students' internal desire to learn. For an inspirational discussion about motivation for engaging students, with a leaning toward the intrinsic perspective, see Tara Garcia Mathewson's (2019) "How to Unlock Students' Internal Drive for Learning."

De-stressing before Engagement in HITS via Prior Knowledge

Some stress can have a positive impact on learning because it keeps students piqued, emotionally and cognitively, when they are engaged in HITS. Individuals, however, might experience intense stress before taking tests, making presentations, or engaging in challenging assignments. These students benefit from educators who recognize the impact of stress on learning and the need for helping students to relax and concentrate so that anticipating a potentially frustrating encounter is replaced with embracing a potentially growth-oriented experience. Noting this difference is more than playing with semantics because stress is real and can be detrimental or beneficial for learning.

Graphic organizers can help because they connect naturally with the human brain's love of making connections to concepts, topics, and themes. Yes, the brain loves to structure information which increases its capacity to better understand and retain information. Examples of graphic organizers include semantic maps, semantic feature analysis grids, concept maps, character maps, K-W-L charts for informational text, Venn diagrams, comparison-contrast matrixes, structured (hierarchical) overviews, anticipation guides, and other structures. Some of these graphic organizers are presented in the "Promoting Critical Thinking" chapter of this book, and others are available via Internet websites. Using them promotes natural and effective connections to the brain's system of processing information, and they are especially pertinent when complex vocabulary and ideas are presented. Simultaneously, the brain's stress level might be reduced because this essential information is organized, connected, and clarified on the graphic organizers as learners build and activate knowledge before, during, and after experiencing challenging material. An interesting perspective on prior knowledge is that it not only consists of intellectual, rational, and academic (cognitive) components but also includes emotional, social, and dispositional (affective) behaviors. Nine decades ago, Bartlett (1932) posited that prior knowledge and recall (or re-creation) of material are based on cognition, interest, attitude, culture, and the social context. Bartlett believed that focusing on literal recall is limited, and even dysfunctional, and that constructive remembering is necessary because the environment changes and requires constructive and flexible adjustments.

> So-called "literal," or accurate, recall is an artificial construction ... Even if it could be secured, in the enormous majority of instances it would be biologically detrimental. Life is a continuous play of adaptation between changing response and varying environment. Only in a relatively few cases—and those mostly the production of an elaborately guarded civilization— could the retention unchanged of the effects of experience be anything but a hindrance. (Bartlett, 1932, p. 16; see also Lynch, n.d.; Nord, 1995).

Bartlett's perspective is often deemphasized by those who believe independent, rational thinking should restrict the role of emotions during the process of opinion building. Jiménez-Aleixandre and Puig (2012) note, "Although we think that it is desirable for students (and people) to integrate care and empathy in their reasoning, we would contemplate purely or mainly emotive reasoning as less strong than rational reasoning" (p. 1011). Regrettably, this position might suggest that emotionally based reasoning is a threat to rational thinking and that rational thinking processes, by themselves, should not only guide critical thinking instruction but should also ignore emotions during the opinion-building processes. This perspective does not appear to be realistic because expecting students to ignore emotions might actually increase their influence (Lombard, Schneider, Merminod, & Weiss, 2020). The important point is for educators to maintain a balance of respecting students' perspectives, nurturing their open-mindedness, and guiding them to consider different views.

Such a balance has strong potential for increasing learners' prior knowledge and, in turn, decreasing their stress level when approaching challenging activities and assignments. An expected outcome is an increase in empathy, which is defined as "a psychological construct regulated by both cognitive and affective components, producing emotional understanding" (Shamay-Tsoory, Aharon-Peretz, & Perry, 2009, p. 617). Because empathy can have a positive or negative impact on perceiving others' perspectives, cognitive empathy (which relies more on one's complex perspective-taking system) is better positioned for increasing an understanding of the emotional perspectives and reactions of those from different cultures and with different values (Lombard et al., 2020; Sadler & Zeidler, 2005; Young & Koenigs, 2007).

De-stressing before Engagement in HITS via Synchronicity

When students build and activate their affective and cognitive knowledge base, their processing involves inclusive aspects of synchronicity. That is, facets of synchronicity—personal and academic—come together because they simultaneously share a purpose or function so that a specific outcome is achieved. To assume otherwise is to suggest that we only have the capacity to learn, store, and use information in fragmented memories devoid of the situational context in which they occurred. Whether students are attempting to solve rational inequalities in mathematics or trying to interpret stream-of-consciousness literature in English, related memories are apt to include the challenging task as well as the frustration, joy, or feeling of accomplishment. Dispositions—mood, temperament, outlook, spirit—emerge during teaching and learning, and sensitivity to this perspective on synchronicity can help to reduce stress.

When we become interested in extending synchronicity to our earthly and spiritual lives, we might initially question so-called (meaningless) coincidences and déjà vus; however, with experience and reflection, we might eventually grow to understand that these events have a meaningful purpose that affect our current and future lives and bring us together as a worldwide web of community. Furthermore, analytical psychiatrist Carl Jung advanced his theory of synchronicity, referred to as the collective unconscious, as he believed that events in people's lives can reflect meaningful coincidences. In *Jung on Synchronicity and the Paranormal*, Robert Main (1999/2005) clarifies aspects of Jung's major contribution to this theoretical and controversial area. Considering these perspectives, of course, reflects the beauty of choice as people accept, reject, or mediate the value of synchronicity in their personal and academic lives. In addition to Main's contribution, other supportive insights are provided in Kenneth Harris's (2019) *Synchronicity: The Magic, the Mystery, and the Meaning* and in Warren Malkoff's (2019) *Peace to Pieces to Peace: My Cross-Cultural Journey*.

Interestingly, during a January 2021 visit to the Huntington, NY, Heckscher Museum of Art, visitors were drawn to Chris Ann Ambery's three beautiful works of art titled *Hope, 2020*; *Lean on Me II, 2020*; and *Contemplations, 2019*. What follows are her reflections on her art:

> I have always been intrigued by the evanescence of memory. For a brief moment in time, a thought, idea, person, or thing can be all-consuming. Eventually, this

will fade away into the recess of our memory, seemingly forgotten until something triggers it, and once again, it is brought to the surface. My work is ... a journey into the residual memories and emotions that have been imprinted in me from my experiences. As I work, intuition takes over, and I think through my hands. Although many times I begin with an idea or intention, as my work progresses, I allow it to take me on a journey. I am never certain of what the final outcome will be.

Sharing Ambery's reflection as well as Harris's, Malkoff's, and Main's poignant and substantive insights might help others to understand that solving problems (including artistic decision-making) is not an exact process, that synchronizing previous experiences with current realities has spiritual and earthly value, and that discovering or rediscovering an "inner calm" can reduce stress and increase meaningful productivity. Before progressing to the next section of this chapter, reflect on the Flower of Life symbol in Figure 7.1.

De-stressing before Engagement in HITS via Relaxation Techniques

Other holistic approaches are also effective for de-stressing. By practicing relaxation techniques several minutes each day in the classroom and at home, students and teachers can discover their reserve of inner calm. Corless (2019), executive editor of the *Harvard Heart Letter*, suggests six relaxation techniques that can reduce stress by evoking the relaxation response. Two of these techniques are adapted here: mindfulness meditation, for example, might be helpful for people with pain, depression, and anxiety; it involves sitting comfortably, focusing on breathing, and bringing one's attention to the current moment. Repetitive prayer is another technique that might be appealing to those who consider spirituality or religion to be meaningful in their lives; while focusing on

Reflections on Critical Thinking ◆ 99

Figure 7.1 Flower of Life

breathing, individuals can silently repeat a short prayer or a phrase of a prayer.

Because prayer is personal and intimate, Malkoff suggests his version of a Navajo prayer, which is adapted here:

> *Walking in the Beauty Way*
> *I walk with beauty.*
> *I walk with beauty above me.*
> *I walk with beauty behind me.*
> *I walk with beauty all around me.*

Students might consider meditating on this prayer, or one of the lines in it, or selecting a different culturally based prayer that reflects personal meaning. Whatever the belief, prayer is important because it tunes out the noise and calms the person (Wisneski, 2021).

A variation of these relaxation techniques are Dan Harris's (2014) approaches to mindfulness meditation, which can reduce stress and increase engagement. Harris suggests getting started with just five minutes a day of meditation, which includes (1) sitting with your spine straight and your eyes closed; (2) focusing your full attention on the feeling of your breadth inhaling and exhaling through your nose, chest, or belly; (3) realizing that as your mind wonders, focus your attention back to your breath.

These and similar approaches support students as whole people, not just receptacles to be filled with academic knowledge. Students respond meaningfully to most teaching and learning contexts when teachers realize that the best way to enter their heads is through their hearts. Considering students' emotional and social needs has potential to reduce their stress, to open their hearts, and to calm their minds for the challenges of life, including engagement in HITS. This suggests, "Synchronicity holds promise that if we want to change inside, the patterns of our external life will change as well" (Jean Shinoda Bolen, cited in Harris, 2019).

8
In Retrospect

Connections and applications of critical thinking to subject content are highlighted in this book because they are essentially more effective than teaching critical thinking generically (Willingham, 2019). Students seem to benefit from direct instruction as they learn, practice, and apply critical thinking across the curriculum (Bangert-Drowns & Bankert, 1990). Students also develop critical thinking skills when instruction highlights complex problem solving, classroom dialogue and discussion, and mentoring (Abrami, et al., 2015; Goodwin, 2017).

Furthermore, this book does not impose didactic approaches on teachers. Instead, they are encouraged to choose from a number of thoughtful strategies and activities, including some of those presented here, that support direct instruction and student-centered learning and their application to content. This balanced approach is more likely to result in transfer of learning when it is well matched with the purposes, goals, and objectives of subject content as well as the strengths, interests, and needs of students.

While seemingly a stretch to the critical thinking process, we can perceive our mission and ourselves as "divine craftspersons" who continue to support critical thinking as a spiritual service to our neighbors and to humanity as a whole (John Paul II, 1999). Regardless of our positions in society—artists, scientists, workers, technicians, witnesses of the faith, professionals, mothers, fathers, teachers—we need to accept a major responsibility of supporting critical thinking as an essential social service in favor of the common good. Although Pope John Paul II (1999) did not specifically address the issue of critical thinking, he did inspire us to develop our creative talents in ways that enrich cultural heritage and all humanity. In this pragmatic context, we need to help students to master critical thinking as an artful synthesis of theoretical (and spiritual) knowledge and practical experience in the development of exceptional judgment (Samet, 2015). Francis Bacon's (1597) essay "Of Studies" also supported the sensible mix of learning and practical experience. "Read not to contradict and refute; nor to believe and take for granted; nor to find talk and discourse; but to weigh and consider."

Another potential stretch is worth considering: the deeper the connection to critical thinking, the greater the link to a Buberian I-Thou (Buber, 1923/1937/1970; see also Brooks, 2016; Donnelly, 2016; Richards, 2017). To understand the essence of I-Thou, it is important to distinguish I-It and I-Thou attitudes toward the world. Briefly described, I-It represents necessary realities that most people experience, such as security, safety, sureness, and other details and responsibilities of life; however, I-Thou reflects deeper and intimate responses, such as understanding and feeling for others. Both I-It and I-Thou attitudes can be experienced separately or can be connected meaningfully, as in dealing with the details and responsibilities of helping children with disabilities to think critically and, simultaneously, demonstrating genuine caring for them as whole people. From an inclusive perspective, Buber would argue that relationships between teachers and students should not be limited by pre-established and categorized needs (Veck, 2012). Inevitably, the situational context of collaborative dialogue is important, as I-It relationships can negatively result in treating people as objects to exploit, and I-Thou relationships can positively result in treating people with full spiritual respect.

This book has highlighted interactive considerations for maintaining an open-minded mindset, working collaboratively, developing a sense of belonging, and reaching consensus. Although these are important collective concerns, they should not negate the value of independent thinking because sometimes "groupthink can lead to unhealthy decision-making patterns. Like egocentric thinking, it is difficult to overcome. Breaking the cycle requires individuals to stand apart from the group and question opinions, thoughts, and popular ideas. This can be especially difficult for adolescents, but teachers can play a key role in encouraging independent thought and action in students" (Wabisabi Learning, n.d.).

The importance of independent thinking is noted in everyday experiences, including in the media. A classic example is the 1957 award-winning film *12 Angry Men*. This American court room drama reveals the backroom, intense interactions of 12 white jurors as they deliberate the fate of an ethnic minority teenager accused of murdering his father. As the jurors deliberate the 18-year-old's conviction or acquittal, they reveal their personalities, biases, and eagerness to judge the Puerto Rican teenager. The film provides an excellent reminder (and role model) of how the strength and empowerment of one dissenting jury member can elicit change.

When students, individually and collectively, demonstrate the *dynamis* to think critically, they experience a transformation that initially can result in discord because the birth of a "new path" to thinking requires the death of antiquated habits of thinking. Metaphorically, T. S. Elliot's poem "The Journey of the Magi" (All Poetry, n.d.) provides inspiration for this challenging, growth-oriented, psycho-spiritual journey as students pursue a "new road" to thinking that gradually nurtures their confidence and competence in analyzing, synthesizing, applying, and evaluating information related to politics as well as to domestic, national, and international issues. Nurturing students' HITS across the curriculum and through the grades will increase their chances of becoming morally sensitive and rationally independent thinkers and informed citizens whose open-minded behavior is modeled and emulated by peers. So let's begin every school day with profound and spiritual insight:

> MORNING IS GOD'S WAY OF SAYING ONE MORE TIME, GO MAKE A DIFFERENCE, TOUCH A HEART, ENCOURAGE A MIND, INSPIRE A SOUL, AND ENJOY THE DAY.

This daily reminder can transform lives into a spiritual journey and can transfer faith into positive action, both of which are necessary for the survival of our republic.

References

Abla, C. (2019). 7 ways to spark engagement. *Edutopia*. Retrieved from https://www.edutopia.org/article/7-ways-spark-engagement
Abrami, P., Bernard, R., Borokhovski, E., Waddington, D., Wade, C., & Persson, T. (2015). Strategies for teaching students to think critically: A meta-analysis. *Review of Educational Research, 852*(2), 275–314.
Abrami, P., Bernard, R., Borokhovski, E., Wade, A., Surkes, M., Tamim, R., & Zhang, D. (2008). Instructional interventions affecting critical thinking skills and dispositions: A stage 1 meta-analysis. *Review of Educational Research, 78*(4), 1102–1134.
Achieve. (2014). Rising to the challenge: Are high school graduates prepared for college and work? Retrieved from http://www.achieve.org/rising-challenge-powerpoint
Allington, R. (1977). If they don't read, how they ever gonna get good? *Journal of Reading, 21*(1), 57–61.
Allington, R. (2006). *What really matters for struggling readers: Designing research-based programs*. Boston, MA: Pearson.
All Poetry. (n.d.). https://allpoetry.com/The-Journey-Of-The-Magi
Anderson, J., & Freebody, P. (1981). Vocabulary knowledge. In J. Guthrie (Ed.), *Comprehension and teaching: Research review* (pp. 71–117). Newark, DE: International Reading Association.
Anderson, J., & Rainie, L. (2018). The future of well-being in a tech-saturated world. Pew Research Center. Retrieved from https://assets.pewresearch.org/wp-content/uploads/sites/14/2018/04/14154552/PI_2018.04.17_Future-of-Well-Being_FINAL.pdf
Anson, I. (2018). Partisanship, political knowledge, and the Dunning-Kruger effect. *Political Psychology*. Retrieved from https://onlinelibrary.wiley.com/doi/abs/10.1111/pops.12490
Aristotle. (1924/2011). *Rhetoric* (J. H. Freese, Trans.; C. River, Ed.) [iBook version]. Retrieved from https://itunes.apple.com

Armstrong, P. (2020). Bloom's taxonomy. Center for Teaching, Vanderbilt University. Retrieved from https://cft.vanderbilt.edu/guides-sub-pages/blooms-taxonomy/

Aust, P. (1981). Using the life storybook in treatment of children in placement. *Child Welfare, 60*(8), 535–536, 553–560.

Azarian, B. (2018). The Dunning-Kruger effect may help explain Trump's support. *Psychology Today*. Retrieved from https://www.psychologytoday.com/us/blog/mind-in-the-machine/201808/the-dunning-kruger-effect-may-help-explain-trumps-support?eml

Bacon, F. (1597). Of studies. In E. Samet (Ed.), *Leadership: Essential writings by our greatest thinkers* (p. 199). New York: Norton.

Bakewell, S. (2010). *How to live or a life of Montaigne: In one question and twenty attempts at an answer*. UK: Chatto & Windus (Imprint of Random House).

Bangert-Drowns, R. L., & Bankert, E. (1990, April). Meta-analysis of effects of explicit instruction for critical thinking. Paper presented at the annual meeting of the American Educational Research Association, Boston, MA.

Barber, W. (2019). Research is vital to the moral integrity of social movements. Economic Policy Institute. Retrieved from https://www.epi.org/blog/research-is-vital-to-the-moral-integrity-of-social-movements/

Bartlett, F. (1932). *Remembering: A study in experimental and social psychology*. Cambridge, UK: Cambridge University Press.

Bavel, J., & Pereira, A. (2018). The partisan brain: An identity-based model of political belief. *Trends in Cognitive Sciences, 22*(3), 213–224.

Beck, I., McKeown, M., & Kucan, L. (2002). *Bringing words to life: Robust vocabulary instruction*. New York: Guilford Press.

Benedict XVI. (2005). *Deus caritas est*. Retrieved from http://www.vatican.va/content/benedict-xvi/en/encyclicals/documents/hf_ben-xvi_enc_20051225_deus-caritas-est.html

Bennett, H., & Nimoy, L. (1986). *Star Trek IV: The Voyage Home* [Motion Picture]. United States: Paramount Pictures.

Bloom, B., Engelhart, M., Furst, E., Hill, W., & Krathwohl. D. (1956). *Taxonomy of educational objectives: The classification of educational goals. Handbook I: Cognitive* domain. New York: David McKay Company.

Bonagura, D. (2019). *Steadfast in faith: Catholicism and the challenges of secularism*. Providence, RI: Cluny Media.

Borel, B. (2018). Clicks, lies, and videotape. *Scientific American, 319*(4), 39–43.

Boyd, M., & Fales, W. (1983). Reflective learning: Key to learning from experience. *Journal of Humanistic Psychology, 23*(2), 99–117.

Brooks, D. (2016). I-Thou v I-It relationships. *The Straits Times*. Retrieved from https://www.straitstimes.com/opinion/i-thou-v-i-it-relationships

Brookshire, B. (2019). *Using art to show the threat of climate change*. Retrieved from https://www.sciencenewsforstudents.org/article/using-art-show-climate-change-threat

Buber, M. (1923/1937/1970). *I and Thou*. New York: Simon & Schuster.
Buehl, D. (2014). *Classroom strategies for interactive learning*. Newark, DE: International Literacy Association.
Building Critical Thinking. (2013). Retrieved from https://building criticalthinking.com/rhetoric/
Calderon, V., & Yu, D. (2017). Student enthusiasm falls as high school graduation nears. Retrieved from https://news.gallup.com/opinion/gallup/211631/student-enthusiasm-falls-high-school-graduation-nears.aspx
Cambourne, B. (1999). Conditions for literacy learning: Turning learning theory into classroom instruction. A mini-case study. *The Reading Teacher*, 54(4), 414–429.
Canestrari, C., Branchini, E., Bianchi, I., Savardi, U., & Burro, R. (2018). Pleasures of the mind: What makes jokes and insight problems enjoyable. *Frontiers in Psychology, 8*. Retrieved from https://www.frontiersin.org/articles/10.3389/fpsyg.2017.02297/full
CCESI. (2020). Critical thinking and reflective practice. Center for Civic Engagement and Social Impact. Retrieved from https://www.wcupa.edu/_services/civicEngagementSocialImpact/facultyReflection.aspx
Corless, J. (2019). Six relaxation techniques to reduce stress: Practicing even a few minutes per day can provide a reserve of inner calm. Harvard Health Publishing, Harvard Medical School. Retrieved from https://www.health.harvard.edu/mind-and-mood/six-relaxation-techniques-to-reduce-stress
Countryman, J. (2012). *Two ways to think or Montaigne and Freud on the human paradox*. Unpublished honors thesis, Florida State University, Tallahassee, Florida.
Cramer, J., & Huber, K. (2016). Using politics to teach critical thinking. *Eschool News*. Retrieved from https://www.eschoolnews.com/2016/12/01/politics-teach-critical-thinking/
Cuesta College. (2021). *Critical thinking: Recognizing propaganda techniques and errors of faulty logic*. Retrieved from https://www.cuesta.edu/student/resources/ssc/study_guides/critical_thinking/103_think_logic_errors.html
Culp, D. (2018). Can faith coexist with reason? *Faith Magazine*. Retrieved from https://faithmag.com/can-faith-coexist-reason
Dalile, L. (2012). How schools are killing creativity. *Huffpost*. Retrieved from https://www.huffpost.com/entry/a-dictator-racing-to-nowh_b_1409138
dePaola, T. (2018). *Quiet*. New York: Simon & Schuster.
Dewey, J. (1933). *How we think*. New York: Heath.
Dewey, J. (1938a). *Experience and education*. New York: Macmillan.
Dewey, J. (1938b). *Logic: The theory of inquiry*. New York: Henry Holt.
Dewey, J. (1944). *Democracy and education*. New York: Free Press.

Donnelly, S. (2016). The antidote to this year's election season: Martin Buber. *RealClearLife*. Retrieved from http://www.realclearlife.com/books/the-antidote-to-this-years-election-season-martin-buber/

Dreweke, J. (2019). Promiscuity propaganda: Access to information and services does not lead to increases in sexual activity. *Guttmacher Policy Review*, 22, 29–36. Retrieved from https://www.guttmacher.org/sites/default/files/article_files/gpr2202919.pdf

Dunning, D. (2011). The Dunning-Kruger effect: On being ignorant of one's own ignorance. In J. Olson & M. Zanna (Eds.), *Advances in experimental social psychology* (vol. 44, pp. 247–296). Atlanta, GA: Elsevier.

Dunning, D. (2016). The psychological quirk that explains why you love Donald Trump. *Politico Magazine*. Retrieved from https://www.politico.com/magazine/story/2016/05/donald-ofcriticalthinking-trump-supporters-dunning-kruger-effect-213904

Dwyer, C.P. (2017). *Critical thinking: Conceptual perspectives and practical guidelines*. Cambridge, UK: Cambridge University Press.

Dwyer, C. (2018). *Strange bedfellows: Creativity and critical thinking: What you thought you knew about creativity in critical thinking*. Retrieved from https://www.psychologytoday.com/us/blog/thoughts-thinking/201803/strange-bedfellows-creativity-critical-thinking

Dwyer, C. (2019). *12 important dispositions for critical thinking: A student-educator negotiated model facilitated through interactive management*. Retrieved from https://www.psychologytoday.com/us/blog/thoughts-thinking/201904/12-important-dispositions-critical-thinking

Dwyer, C., Harney, O., Hogan, M., & Kavanagh, C. (2016). Facilitating a student-educator conceptual model of dispositions towards critical thinking through interactive management. *Educational Technology & Research*, 65, 47–73.

Dyson, M. (2017). *Tears we cannot stop: A sermon to White America*. New York: St. Martin's Press.

Elder, L., & Paul, R. (2010). Critical thinking: Competency standards essential for the cultivation of intellectual skills, part 1. *Journal of Developmental Education*, 34(2), 38–39.

Elfatihi, M. (2017). A rationale for the integration of critical thinking skills in EFL/ESL instruction. *Higher Education of Social Science*, 12(2), 26–31.

Elleman, A., Lindo, E., Morphy, P., & Compton, D. (2009). The impact of vocabulary instruction on passage-level comprehension of school-age children. *Journal of Research on Educational Effectiveness*, 2(1), 1–44.

Eyler, J., Giles, D., & Schmiede. A. (1996). *A practitioner's guide to reflection in service-learning: Student voices and reflections*. Nashville, TN: Vanderbilt University. Retrieved from https://leduccenter.files.wordpress.com/2015/02/practitioners-guide-to-reflection-in-service-learning.pdf

Foundation for Critical Thinking. (2019). *Our concept and definition of critical thinking*. Retrieved from https://www.criticalthinking.org/pages/our-conception-of-critical-thinking/411

Frayer, D., Frederick, W. C., & Klausmeier, H. J. (1969). *A schema for testing the level of cognitive mastery*. Madison, WI: Wisconsin Center for Education Research.

Freire, P. (2000). *Pedagogy of the oppressed* (30th anniv. ed.; M. B. Ramos, Trans.). New York, NY: Continuum.

Frey, N., Fisher, D., & Everlove, S. (2009). *Productive group work: How to engage students, build teamwork, and promote understanding*. Alexandria, VA: ASCD.

Goodwin, B. (2017). Research matters: Critical thinking won't develop through osmosis. *Educational Leadership*, 74(5), 80–81.

Haber, J. (2020a). *Critical thinking*. Cambridge, MA: MIT Press.

Haber, J. (2020b). It's time to get serious about teaching critical thinking." *Inside Higher Ed*. Retrieved from https://www.insidehighered.com/views/2020/03/02/teaching-students-think-critically-opinion

Hammond, J., & Senor, R. (2014). *The mentor: Leading with love, the ultimate resource*. Bloomington, IN: iUniverse.

Harris, D. (2014). *10% happier*. New York: HarperCollins.

Harris, K. (2019). *Synchronicity: The magic, the mystery, the meaning*. York, PA: Capucia.

Hart, B., & Risley, T. (1995). *Meaningful differences in the everyday experiences of young American children*. Baltimore, MD: Brookes.

Heick, T. (2019). *20 types of learning journals that help students think*. Retrieved from https://www.teachthought.com/literacy/20-types-of-learning-journals-that-help-students-think/

Hidden Curriculum. (2014). Rigor. In S. Abbot (Ed.), *The glossary of education reform*. Great Schools Partnership. Retrieved from http://edglossary.org/hidden-curriculum. http://edglossary.org/rigor/

Highet, G. (1950). *The art of teaching*. New York, NY: Knopf.

Hobbs, R., & McGee, S. (2014). Teaching about propaganda: An Examination of the historical roots of media literacy. *Journal of Media Literacy Education*, 6(2), 56–67.

Hoffman, M. (2000). *Empathy and moral development: Implications for caring and justice*. New York: Cambridge University Press.

Hume, D. (1983/1751). *An inquiry concerning the principles of morals*. Indianapolis, IN: Hackett.

Intractor, S., & Kunzman, R. (2006). The person in the profession: Renewing teacher vitality through professional development. *The Educational Forum*, 71(1), 16–32.

IRA Inspire. (2012). Literacy goes pop! Retrieved from www.reading.org

Jewitt, C., & Kress, G. (2003). *Multimodal literacy*. London, UK: Peter Lang Publishing.

Jiménez-Aleixandre, M., & Puig, B. (2012). Argumentation, evidence evaluation and critical thinking. In B. Fraser, K. Tobin, & C. McRobbie (Eds.), *Second international handbook of science education* (pp. 1001–1015). Retrieved from https://doi.org/10.1007/978-1-4020-9041-7_66

John Paul II. (1979). *Redemptor hominis*. Retrieved from http://www.vatican.va/content/john-paul-ii/en/encyclicals/documents/hf_jp-ii_enc_04031979_redemptor-hominis.html

John Paul II. (1999). *Letter of his holiness Pope John Paul II to artists*. Retrieved from https://w2.vatican.va/content/john-paul-ii/en/letters/1999/documents/hf_jp-ii_let_23041999_artists.html

Jones, J. (2021). LGBT identification rises to 5.6% in latest U.S. estimate. Retrieved from https://news.gallup.com/poll/329708/lgbt-identification-rises-latest-estimate.aspx

Juliani, A.J. (2019). 10 design thinking activities to get your group creating. Retrieved from http://ajjuliani.com/design-thinking-activities/

Just Add Students. (2020). Propaganda and critical thinking. Retrieved from https://justaddstudents.com/propaganda/

Kahneman, D. (2011). *Thinking, fast and slow*. New York: Farrar, Straus, and Giroux.

Kameli, S., & Baki, R. (2013). The impact of vocabulary knowledge level on EFL reading comprehension. *International Journal of Applied Linguistics and English Literature*, 2(1), 85–89.

Kasten, G. (2017). Overcoming obstacles to critical thinking. *Edutopia*. Retrieved from https://www.edutopia.org/blog/critical-thinking-necessary-skill-g-randy-kasten

Kelly, K., Laminack, L., & Gould, E. (2020). Confronting bias with children's literature: A preservice teacher's journey to developing a critical lens for reading the word and the world. *The Reading Teacher*, 74(3), 297–304.

Kelly, L., & Moses, L. (2018). Children's literature that sparks inferential discussions. *The Reading Teacher*, 72(1), 21–29.

Kenrick, D., Cohen, A., Neuberg, S., & Gialdini, R. (2018). The science of anti-science thinking. *Scientific American*, 319(1), 36–41.

King, M. L. (1967). *Where do we go from here? Speech delivered at the 11thannual SCLC convention*. Stanford, CA: The Martin Luther King, Jr. Research and Education Institute, Stanford University.

King, P. M., & Kitchener, K. S. (1994). *Developing reflective judgment: Understanding and promoting intellectual growth and critical thinking in adolescents and adults*. San Francisco: Jossey Bass.

Kolluri, S. (2017/2018). Politicizing pedagogy: Teaching for liberty and justice at urban schools. *Phi Delta Kappan*, 99(4), 39–44.

Korovkin, S., & Nikiforova O. (2014). Cognitive and affective mechanisms of creative problem solving facilitation by humor. *Experimental Psychology (Russia)*, 7(4), 37–51.

Korovkin, S., & Nikiforova O. (2015). Humor as a facilitator of insight problem solving. Retrieved from https://www.researchgate.net/profile/Sergei_Korovkin/publication/281782383_Humor_as_a_Facilitator_of_Insight_Problem_Solving/links/59e8f722aca272bc425bee02/Humor-Facilitator-of-Insight-Problem-Solving.pdf

Kress, G. (2010). *Multimodality: A social semiotic approach to contemporary communication*. Abingdon, Oxon, UK: Routledge.

Kruger, J., & Dunning, D. (1999). Unskilled and unaware of it: How difficulties in recognizing one's incompetence lead to inflated self-assessments. *Journal of Personality and Social Psychology, 77*(6), 1121–1134.

Kubovy, M. (1999). On the pleasures of the mind. In D. Kahneman, E. Diener, & D. N. Schwarz (Eds.), *Well-being: The foundations of hedonic psychology* (pp. 134–154). New York, NY: Russell Sage Foundation.

Laminack, L., & Kelly, K. (2019). *Reading to make a difference: Using literature to help students speak freely, think deeply, and take action*. Portsmouth, NH: Heinemann.

Lapp, D., Fisher, D., & Wolsey, T. D. (2009). *Literacy growth for every child: Differentiated small-group instruction K–6*. New York: Guilford.

Little, H. (2018). Media literacy: A moving target. *Knowledge Quest, 47*(1), 16–23.

Lombard, F., Schneider, D., Merminod, M., & Weiss, L. (2020). Balancing emotion and reason to develop critical thinking about popularized neurosciences. *Science & Education, 29*, 1139–1176.

Lotherington, H. (2011). *Pedagogy of multiliteracies: Rewriting Goldilocks*. New York: Routledge.

Lowenstein, L. (1995). The resolution scrapbook as an aid in the treatment of traumatized children. *Child Welfare, 74*(4), 889–904.

Luka, I. (2014). Design thinking in pedagogy. *Journal of Education, Culture, and Society, 2*, 63–74.

Lynch, K. (n.d.). *Rethinking critical thinking: Values and attitudes*. Retrieved from https://tomprof.stanford.edu/posting/510

Main, R. (1999/2005). *Jung on synchronicity and the paranormal*. Princeton, NJ. Princeton University Press; New York, NY: Routledge of Taylor & Francis.

Malkoff, W. (2019). *Peace to pieces to peace: My cross-cultural journey*. Murrells Inlet, SC: Covenant Books.

Manoli, P., & Papadopoulou, M. (2012). Graphic organizers as a reading strategy: Research findings and issues. *Creative Education, 3*(3), 348–356. Retrieved from http://www.SciRP.org/journal/ce

Marlatt, R., & Dallacqua, A. (2019). Loud and clear: Using the graphic novel to challenge the status quo in content area literacy. *Journal of Language and Literacy Education, 15*(1), 1–24.

Martens, P., Martens, R., Doyle, M., Loomis, J., Fuhrman, L., Stout, R., Soper, E. (2018). Painting writing, writing painting: Thinking, seeing, and problem solving through story. *The Reading Teacher, 71*(6), 669–679.

Martin, R. (2006). *The psychology of humor: An Integrative approach*. Burlington, MA: Elsevier Academic Press.

Marzano, R. (2004). *Building background knowledge for academic achievement: Research on what works in schools*. Alexandria, VA: Association for Supervision and Curriculum Development.

Mathewson, T. (2019). How to unlock students' internal drive for learning. *The Hechinger Report.* Retrieved from https://hechingerreport.org/intrinsic-motivation-is-key-to-student-achievement-but-schools-kill-it/

MCA. (n.d.). *Propaganda: The art of persuasion.* Retrieved from http://home.mca.k12.pa.us/~rumbeld/Propaganda%20Techniques%20and%20Persuasive%20Tactics.pdf

McAvoy, P., & Hess, D. (2013). Classroom deliberation in an era of political polarization. *Curriculum Inquiry, 43*(1), 14–47.

Miller, A. (2017). *Pairing young adult and classic literature in the high school English curriculum.* Unpublished doctoral dissertation, University of Maine. *Electronic Theses and Dissertations.* 2645. Retrieved from http://digitalcommons.library.umaine.edu/etd/2645

Mills, H., & Jennings, L. (2011). Talking about talk: Reclaiming the value and power of literature circles. *The Reading Teacher, 64*(8), 590–598.

Minin-White, D. (2017). *Political speech, doublespeak, and critical thinking skills in American education.* Unpublished thesis, Hamline University, Saint Paul, Minnesota. Student Capstone Projects, 83.

Mitchell, A., Gottfried, J., & Barthel, M. (2017). *Trump, Clinton voters divided in their main source for election news.* Pew Research Center. Retrieved from http://www.journalism.org/2017/01/18/trump-clinton-voters-divided-in-their-main-source-for-election-news/

Mitchell, A., Gottfried, J., Kiley, J., & Matsa, K. (2014). *Political polarization and media habits.* Pew Research Center. Retrieved from http://www.journalism.org/2014/10/21/political-polarization-media-habits/

Montagu, A. (1952). The "go-getter" spirit: Competition thrives on insecurity, works against democracy. *The Christian Register.* Retrieved from https://www.harvardsquarelibrary.org/biographies/ashley-montagu-anthropologist-and-social-biologist/

Morawski, C. (2012). Inquiring into the possibilities of multimodal novel study: Teacher candidates respond to *Whirligig* with resolution scrapbooks. *Journal of Adolescent and Adult Literacy, 55*(5), 405–416.

Mueller, T. (2019a). *Crisis of conscience: Whistleblowing in an age of fraud.* New York: Penguin Random House.

Mueller, T. (2019b). Sounding the alarm: Why whistleblowing is an American tradition—and a bad sign. *Time, 59.*

Murillo, L., & Schall, J. (2016). "They didn't teach us well": Mexican-origin students speak out about their readiness for college literacy. *Journal of Adolescent and Adult Literacy, 60*(3), 315–323.

Murray-Everett, N., & Coffield, E. (2020). News-group Fridays: Engaging students in current events. *Social Studies and the Young Learner, 33*(2), 2–8.

Nagy, W. & Scott, J. (2000). Vocabulary processes. In M. Kamil, P. Mosenthal, P. Pearson, & R. Barr (Eds.), *Handbook of reading research* (pp. 269–284). Mahwah, NJ: Erlbaum.

Natanson, H. (2019). Virginia school system to allow students day off to protest. Retrieved from https://www.washingtonpost.com/local/education/one-of-the-nations-biggest-school-systems-will-let-students-take-time-off-to-protest-the-conservative-backlash-has-begun/2019/12/26/7c2ebaf8-27e3-11ea-9c21-2c2a4d2c2166_story.html

National Geographic. (2017). Special issue: Gender revolution. *National Geographic, 231*(1), 1–154.

NBSS. (n.d.). Frayer model and Marzano's six steps to effective vocabulary instruction, pp. 1–14. Retrieved from https://www.nbss.ie/sites/default/files/publications/frayer_model_-vocbulary_strategy_handout__copy_3.pdf

NCSS. (2013). *College, career, and civic life (C3) framework for social studies state standards: Guidance for enhancing the rigor of K-12 civics, economics, geography, and history.* Silver Spring, MD: NCSS. Retrieved from https://www.socialstudies.org/c3

NCSS. (2016). Media literacy (position statement). *Social Education, 73*(4), 183–185.

Nilson, L. (2018). Teaching critical thinking: Some practical points. *Faculty Focus.* Retrieved from https://www.facultyfocus.com/articles/effective-teaching-strategies/teaching-criticalthinking-practical-points/

Noddings, N. (2013/1984). *Caring: A relational approach to ethics and moral education.* Berkeley: University of California Press.

Noddings, N., & Brooks, L. (2017). *Teaching controversial issues: The case for critical thinking and moral commitment in the classroom.* New York: Teachers College Press.

Nord, N. (1995). *Religion & American education.* Chapel Hill, NC: University of North Carolina Press.

NYSED. (n.d.). *Culturally responsive sustaining education.* Retrieved from http://www.nysed.gov/common/nysed/files/programs/crs/culturally-responsive-sustaining-education-framework.pdf

Obama, B. (2014). *My brother's keeper.* Retrieved from https://obamawhitehouse.archives.gov/my-brothers-keeper

Palumbo, A., & Sanacore, J. (2013). Serious ideas and middle school students. *The Educational Forum, 77*(2), 192–198.

Paul, R., & Elder, L. (2007). *A guide to educators: Critical thinking competency standards.* Foundation for Critical Thinking Press. Retrieved from https://www.criticalthinking.org/files/SAM_Comp%20Stand_07opt.pdf

Pousley, B. (2017). *Exploring design thinking in the classroom.* Teaching and Learning Lab. Cambridge, MA: Harvard Graduate School of Education. Retrieved from https://tll.gse.harvard.edu/blog/exploring-design-thinking-classroom

Protheroe, N. (2004). Research report: Motivating reluctant learners. *Principal, 84*(1), 46–48.

Rauth, I., Koppen, E., Jobst, B., & Meinel, C. (2010). Design thinking: An educational model towards creative confidence. First international conference on design creativity. Hasso-Plattner Design Thinking Research Program, Hasso-Plattner-Institut für Softwaresystemtechnik GmbH, Germany.

Reznitskaya, A., & Wilkinson, A. (2017). *The most reasonable answer: Helping students build better arguments together.* Boston, MA: Harvard Education Press.

Reznitskaya, A., & Wilkinson, A. (2017/2018). Truth matters: Teaching young students to search for the most reasonable answer. *Phi Delta Kappan, 99*(4), pp. 33–38.

Richards, J. (2017). You and I, I and It: Martin Buber's I and thou. *Epoché Philosophy Monthly.* Retrieved from https://epochemagazine.org/you-and-i-i-and-it-martin-buber-3938ec11785d?gi=990e8abd5311

Rodgers, C. (2002). Defining reflection: Another look at John Dewey and reflective thinking. *Teachers College Record, 104*(4), 842–866.

Rowe, M., Gillespie, B., Harris, K., Koether, S., Shannon, L., & Rose, L. (2015). Redesigning a general education science course to promote critical thinking. *Cell Biology Education, 14*(3). 1–12.

Sadler, T., & Zeidler, D. (2005). Patterns of informal reasoning in the context of socioscientific decision making. *Journal of Research in Science Teaching, 42*(1), 112–138.

Samet, E. (Ed.). (2015). *Leadership: Essential writings of our greatest thinkers.* New York: Norton.

Sanacore, J. (1999). Improving students' literacy learning through caring relationships with adults. *ENCOUNTER: Education for Meaning and Social Justice, 12*, 13–22.

Sanacore, J. (2004). Genuine caring and literacy learning for African American children. *The Reading Teacher, 57*(8), 744–753.

Sanacore, J. (2005). Increasing student participation in the language arts. *Intervention in School and Clinic, 41*(2), 99–104.

Sanacore, J. (2006). Nurturing lifetime readers. *Childhood Education, 83*(1), 33–37.

Sanacore, J. (2008). Turning reluctant learners into inspired learners. *The Clearing House, 82*(1), 40–44.

Sanacore, J. (2012). Showing children that we care about their literacy learning. *Preventing School Failure, 56*(3), 188–195.

Sanacore, J. (2013). Slow down, you move too fast: Literature circles as reflective practice. *The Clearing House, 86*(3), 116–120.

Sanacore, J. (2017). Will Obama's My Brother's Keeper and similar initiatives have a positive impact on low-income students? *The Clearing House, 90*(4), 152–158.

Sanacore, J., & Palumbo, A. (2010). Middle school students need more opportunities to read across the curriculum. *The Clearing House, 83*(5), 180–185.

Sanacore, J., & Palumbo, A. (2015). A high school diploma doesn't guarantee college success. Commentary. *Education Week 34*(28), 22–23, 25.

Sanacore, J., & Piro, J. (2014). Multimodalities, neuroenhancement, and literacy learning. *International Journal of Progressive Education, 10*(2), 56–72.

Schwartz, R. (1998). Learning to learn vocabulary in content area textbooks. *Journal of Reading, 32*(2), 108–118.

Schwartz, R., & Raphael, T. (1985). Concept of definition: A key to improving students' vocabulary. *The Reading Teacher, 39*(2), 198–205.

Scott, S. (2010). Enhancing reflection skills through learning portfolios: An empirical test. *Journal of Management Education, 34*(3), 430–457.

Sedita, J. (2005). Effective vocabulary instruction. *Insights on Learning Disabilities, 2*(1), 33–45.

Servant, E. (2019). Blessing our complicated life. *The grand miracle: Daily reflections for the season of Advent.* Worcester, PA: Christian History Institute.

Shamay-Tsoory, S. G., Aharon-Peretz, J., & Perry, D. (2009). Two systems for empathy: A double dissociation between emotional and cognitive empathy in inferior frontal gyrus versus ventromedial prefrontal lesions. *Brain: A Journal of Neurology, 132*(Pt 3), 617–627.

Shore, K. (2001). Motivating unmotivated students. *Principal, 81*(2), 16–18, 20.

Smith, B. (2021). Propaganda. *Encyclopedia Britannica.* Retrieved from https://www.britannica.com/topic/propaganda

Snow, C. (2013). Cold versus warm close reading: Building students' stamina for struggling with text. *Reading Today, 30*(6), 18–19.

Spencer, J. (2019). Five ways humor boosts creative thinking and problem-solving. Retrieved from https://spencerauthor.com/humor-boosts-creativity/

Stearns, C. (2020). Graphic novel discussion questions. Retrieved from https://study.com/academy/lesson/graphic-novel-discussion-questions.html

Sternberg, R. J. (2005). Raising the achievement of all students: Teaching for successful intelligence. *Educational Psychology Review, 14*(4), 383–393.

Stevens, K., & Baumtrog, M. (2018) Reason and rhetoric in the time of alternative facts. *Informal Logic, 38*(1). Retrieved from https://informallogic.ca/index.php/informal_logic/issue/view/484

Sulzberger, A. (2018). Our publisher on trust and integrity. *The New York Times,* A1.

Takacs, D. (2003). How does your positionality bias your epistemology? *Thought & Action, 19*(1), 27–38.

Thayer-Bacon, B. (1993). Caring and its relationship to critical thinking. *Educational Theory, 43,* 323–340.

United Nations Educational, Scientific, and Cultural Organization. (2017). Reading the past, writing the future: Fifty years of promoting literacy. Retrieved from https://unesdoc.unesco.org/ark:/48223/pf0000247563

UVM. (n.d.). *Propaganda techniques to recognize.* Retrieved from https://www.uvm.edu/~jleonard/AGRI183/propoaganda.html

Vaca, J., Lapp, D., & Fisher, D. (2011). Designing and assessing productive group work in secondary schools. *Journal of Adolescent and Adult Literacy*, *54*(5), 372–375.

Vaughn, L. (2017). *Living philosophy. A historical introduction to philosophical ideas*. New York: Oxford University Press.

Veck, W. (2012). Martin Buber's concept of inclusion as a critique of special education. *International Journal of Inclusive Education*, *17*(6), 614–628.

Venn, J. (1880). On the diagrammatic and mechanical representations of propositions and reasonings. *Dublin Philosophical Magazine and Journal of Science*, *9*, 1–18.

Vygotsky, L. S. (1978). *Mind in society: The development of higher psychological processes* (M. Cole, V. John-Steiner, S. Scribner, & E. Souberman, Eds. & Trans.). Cambridge, MA: Harvard University Press.

Wabisabi Learning. (n.d.). 7 critical thinking barriers and how to overcome them. Retrieved from https://wabisabilearning.com/blogs/critical-thinking/critical-thinking-barriers

Walton, D. (1998). *The new dialectic: Conversational contexts of argument*. Toronto, Canada: University of Toronto Press.

West, T. (2019). Channeling students' passion for sports into social awareness and bringing change. *EdSurge*. Retrieved from https://www.edsurge.com/news/2019-01-07-channeling-studentspassion-for-sports-into-social-awareness-and-bringing-change

Willingham, D. (2019). How to teach critical thinking. *Education: Future Frontiers, Occasional Paper Series*. Retrieved from https://education.nsw.gov.au/our-priorities/innovate-for-the-future/education-for-a-changing-world/media/documents/exar/How-to-teach-critical-thinking-Willingham.pdf

Wiman, C. (2016). I will love you in the summertime: *The American Scholar*. Retrieved from https://theamericanscholar.org/i-will-love-you-in-the-summertime/

Winograd, K. (2003). The functions of teacher emotions: The good, the bad, and the ugly. *Teachers College Record*, *105*, 1641–1673.

Wisneski, M. (2021, March). Power of prayer. *AARP Magazine*, p. 7.

Yopp, H., & Yopp, R. (2006). *Literature-based reading activities*. Boston: Pearson Education.

Young, L., & Koenigs, M. (2007). Investigating emotion in moral cognition: A review of evidence from functional neuroimaging and neuropsychology. *British Medical Bulletin*, *84*(1), 69–79.

About the Author

Dr. Joseph Sanacore is a journalist, researcher, and professor in the Department of Teaching and Learning at the Post Campus of Long Island University, Brookville, NY. He has authored more than 100 articles, essays, and book chapters. He also was an elementary, middle, and high school teacher and a K–12 language arts and literacy administrator. In addition, he has served as a consultant to school systems nationwide. Dr. Sanacore also was appointed Literacy Program Director for the Annenberg and Rockefeller Foundations' Comprehensive School-Reform Collaboration with the LIU Post College of Education, the Yale University School Development Program, and ethnic minority school districts. He is committed to social justice issues, including the value of teaching critical thinking as an essential support system for the survival of our republic.

Printed in the United States
by Baker & Taylor Publisher Services